I WISH I HAD SAID THAT...

John J. Quinn

All rights reserved. No part of this book shall be reproduced or transmitted in any form or by any means, electronic, mechanical, magnetic, photographic including photocopying, recording or by any information storage and retrieval system, without prior written permission of the publisher. No patent liability is assumed with respect to the use of the information contained herein. Although every precaution has been taken in the preparation of this book, the publisher and author assume no responsibility for errors or omissions. Neither is any liability assumed for damages resulting from the use of the information contained herein.

Copyright © 1998 by John J Quinn

ISBN 978-0-7414-0026-0

Printed in the United States of America

Published November 2002

INFINITY PUBLISHING
1094 New DeHaven Street, Suite 100
West Conshohocken, PA 19428-2713
Toll-free (877) BUY BOOK
Local Phone (610) 941-9999
Fax (610) 941-9959
Info@buybooksontheweb.com
www.buybooksontheweb.com

Dear Reader,

I hope you enjoy this book. It is a compilation of sayings, quotes, poems and facts which have captured my attention. Maybe you will find something that enhances your life or assists in making your day easier. You may want to memorize, analyze and discuss its text with others.

Thank you

John Quinn

Live your life as though your next breath
might be your last.
JOHN QUINN

When we're young, we want to change the world.
When we're old, we want to change the young.
BILL LYON

He who angers me, conquers me.
ANON.

The greatest form of revenge is forgiveness.
ANON.

A fool will lose tomorrow, reaching back for yesterday.
DIONNE WARWICK

Nothing can bring you peace, but yourself.
RALPH WALDO EMERSON

The responsibility for your condition is in your hands.
JOE CLARK

Self-responsibility is the brick and mortar of success.
JOE CLARK

Talk to a man about himself and he will listen for hours.
DISREALI

The art of being happy lies in the power of extracting
happiness from common things.
H. W. BEECHER

Nothing is wasted through failure,
we learn a needed lesson in humility.
ANON.

It is better to have loved and lost,
than not to have loved at all.
TENNYSON

The beginning of corruption is wanting things.
CUS D'AMATO

All true love begins with self-love.
JOHN BRADSHAW

We have to know how to value ourselves
before we can value others.
JOHN BRADSHAW

Time moves quickly, you go overnight from playing
in the all-star game to playing in the old-timers game.
FORMER MAJOR LEAGUER

Children are God's way of telling us
that the world deserves to go on.
CLAUDE LEWIS

Real humor comes from pain.
Humor is the teddy bear that gets us through the night.
LINDA ELLERBEE

We were rich in all aspects of life, except money.
RICH McPHERSON

When we lose the power
of the written word, we lose everything.
TOM BOSWELL

The best way to show gratitude for a gift
is to use that gift.
BOB KORECK

Unfortunately the good times don't last forever.
Fortunately the bad times don't last forever.
KAREEM ABDUL JABBAR

Luck is opportunity meeting preparedness.
ANON.

Coaching's most difficult problem:
To adapt to what he has
instead of forcing what he has to adapt.
BILL LYON

<u>A GREAT COACH</u>
He can take his and beat yours,
and then take yours and beat his.
BUM PHILLIPS

<u>ON DON SHULA</u>
Now he sees the gray between the black and white.
TIM FOLEY

When you win, say little,
When you lose, say less.
BRUCE SMITH - BILLS

The greatest gift that my father gave us nine kids
was the fact that he truly loved our mother.
WES UNSELD

Maybe someday they'll give a war
and nobody will show up.
CARL SANDBURG

Old habits, die hard.
ANON.

Any happiness you get you've got to make yourself.
ALICE WALKER

Poverty is no excuse for failure.
MEL BLOUNT

The bankrupt person
is the one who has lost his enthusiasm.
H. W. ARNOLD

Sandwich criticism between layers of praise.
MARY KAY

We do not feel confident when we are living a lie.
ANNE WILSON SCHAEF

Doylestown, PA. - The day the public library opened, the first two cards were issued to:
1) James Michener
2) Margaret Meade

Anyone can make a mistake.
A fool insists on repeating it.
ROBERT W. MAYNARD

The fear of death keeps us from living, not from dying.
PAUL C. ROUD

A dog wags its tail with its heart.
MARTIN BUXBAUM

Anger is a wind which blows out the lamp of the mind.
ROBERT G. INGERSOLL

If you risk nothing, then you risk everything.
GEENA DAVIS

The value of marriage is not that adults produce children, but that children produce adults.
ANON.

Being a Philosopher, I have a problem for every solution.
ROBERT ZEND

The less you open your heart to others,
the more your heart suffers.
DEEPAK CHOPRA.

The secret to managing a ballclub is to keep the five guys who hate you away from the five guys who aren't sure.
CASEY STENGEL

I have failed over and over in this life, and that is why I succeed.
MICHAEL JORDAN

Pity me the heart that is slow to learn what the quick mind sees at every turn.
EDNA ST. VINCENT MILLAY

That side will win the war, which first runs out of paper.
GEN. HAN SPIEDEL - GERMANY

Whoever said "Its not whether you win or lose that counts", probably lost.
MARTINA NAVRATILOVA

No valor la pena
Nothing is worth the grief.
SPANISH PROVERB

All the sympathy in the world is absolutely worthless.
R. M. THOMSON

I feel that less than 1% of all the people in the world reach their full potential.
BERRY GORDY

An oral agreement isn't worth the paper it's printed on.
ANON.

Razors pain you; river's are damp; acids stain you; and drugs cause cramp. Guns aren't lawful; nooses give; gas smells awful; you might as well live.
DOROTHY PARKER

If you obey all the rules, you miss all the fun.
KATHERINE HEPBURN

When the legend becomes fact, print the legend.
ANON.

It is not as good with money, as it is bad without it.
ANON.

The most devastating state of mind is the absence of hope.
SIDNEY POITIER

Men sitting around talking about bulls, is not the same as one man in the bullring.
ANON.

You celebrate victory, but you analyze defeat.
BILL WALTON

Regret for the things we did can be tempered by time; it is regret for the things we did not do that is inconsolable.
SIDNEY HARRIS

The two most difficult things to handle -
success and failure.
BILL LYON

Beware the man of one book.
THE ROMANS

The trick is growing up without growing old.
CASEY STENGEL

Nothing can resist the power of an idea
whose time has come.
VICTOR HUGO

No one can make you feel inferior without your consent.
ELEANOR ROOSEVELT

All knowledge is remembering.
SOCRATES

If you want to be a writer; read at least one thousand
words for each one you write.
ANON.

Every unhappy family is unhappy in its own way.
TOLSTOY

It was fear that first made Gods in the world.
STATIUS

Beware the fury of a patient man.
DRYDEN

Genius is one percent inspiration
and ninety-nine percent perspiration.
THOMAS EDISON

Hatred is unending fear.
ANON.

Home is the place where, when you have to go there,
they have to take you in.
ROBERT FROST

Hope springs eternal in the human breast.
ALEXANDER POPE

You miss 100% of the shots you don't take.
WAYNE GRETZKY

God gives every bird food ---
but He doesn't throw it into the nest.
LEO J. LATZ, III

The time will come when winter will ask you
what you were doing over the summer.
ANON.

Whatever the mind of man can conceive and believe ---
it can achieve.
NAPOLEON HILL

Success consists of doing
the common things uncommonly well.
ANON.

All our dreams can come true ---
if we have the courage to pursue them.
WALT DISNEY

Few things are harder to put up with than the
annoyance of a good example.
MARK TWAIN

Nothing so needs reforming as other peoples habits.
MARK TWAIN

Television; the more you watch, the less you'll
accomplish.
TED TURNER

It's a terrible thing for a mind to grow up in a slum, but
it is a far worse thing for a slum to grow up in a mind.
CLAUDE LEWIS

Once you start self-pity, you're dead. You're in the
box. I didn't allow myself to go in that -- box. That's
the message. Don't accept it. Keep going!
TINA TURNER

I was the toast of two continents;
Greenland and Antarctica.
DOROTHY PARKER

He has no enemies and none of his friends like him.
OSCAR WILDE

My books are water, books of great geniuses are wine, everybody drinks water.
MARK TWAIN

I have never learned anything except from people younger than myself.
OSCAR WILDE

I sometimes make mistakes, but I am never wrong.
JIMMY HOFFA

He was never better than when the water was up to his neck.
LOUIS XI OF FRANCE

Adults are obsolete children.
DR. SEUSS

It is only when one accepts the impossible that life becomes worth living.
JOAN OF ARC

History is a nightmare from which I am trying to awake.
EUGENE O'NEILL

It is good to know your own business, not anyone else's, and mind it.
GERTRUDE STEIN

The evil that men do lives after them.
The good is oft interred with their bones.
SHAKESPEARE

Don't trouble trouble, till trouble troubles you.
DOLLY PARTON

A life is not worth much, unless it impacts on other lives.
TOMBSTONE
JACKIE R. ROBINSON

Education is the seed of knowledge and wisdom.
BEVERLY HYMAN

Take risks, a ship in port is safe, but that is not what ships are for.
Sail out to sea and do new things.
ANON.

The most damaging words
in the English language are;
It's always been done that way.
GRACE HOPPER

Celebrity is a tragedy.
WALTER WINCHELL

Intelligence does not need education,
education does not prove intelligence.
ANON.

To truly live, you have to experience both laughter and tears.
EILEEN MARIN

You are the only reason why you cannot succeed.
EDWARD JAMES OLMOS

Life is what happens while we are busy making plans.
CLAUDE LEWIS

Wherever they burn books,
they will also in the end burn people.
HEINRICH HEINE - GERMAN POET

He who saves a single soul, saves the world entirely.
OSCAR SHINDLER

Life is difficult, but not impossible.
AUGUST WILSON

The greatest motivator of all ---
the fear of embarrassment.
TUBBY RAYMOND

Some people by the performance of one act
achieve immortality.
STEVEN SPIELBERG

Modern society is guilty of intellectual treason.
"LORD" of the Tunnels

Doing your best is more important than being the best.
CATHY RIGBY

The worst crime is faking it.
KURT COBAIN

Cancer is a reminder of how short a leash you're on.
JOHN CHANCELLOR

It is difficult to overcome affluence.
KIRK DOUGLAS

You have to get on to the next thing,
before they can catch you for the last thing.
JOAN HOUSEMAN

I am too much of an atheist to believe in a life hereafter,
and just to little a Catholic to commit suicide.
J. D. BARRYMORE

There's no difference between a black snake
and a white snake. They both bite.
THURGOOD MARSHALL

The cat in gloves catches no mice.
BEN FRANKLIN

Total maturity is the beginning of rot.
BROOKS PACY

If we have only one good memory left in our hearts, even that may sometime be the means of saving us.
DOSTOYEVSKY

Use fear as a fuel, it will become one of your best friends.
JOSE TORRES

Macho does not prove mucho.
ZSA ZSA GABOR

You're not in that.
M. ANGELOU

God don't make junk. Drugs & alcohol make junk.
ANON.

Live each moment as if you were prepared to die.
SATYR

Whatever America hopes to bring to pass in the world must first come to pass in the heart of America.
DWIGHT D. EISENHOWER

He who waits to do a great deal of good all at once, will never do anything.
SAMUEL JOHNSON

When you stop giving and offering something to the rest of the world, it's time to turn out the lights.
GEORGE BURNS

Things that hurt --- instruct.
BEN FRANKLIN

Words can offend, regardless of how significant our intent or how noble our purpose.
CLAUDE LEWIS

I'd rather be a free man in the grave, than a puppet or a slave.
JIM BROWN

If you don't enjoy the fight, get out of the ring, because you can't win.
DONALD TRUMP

Never complain, never explain.
PHIL DONAHUE

Takers eat well, givers sleep well.
CHI-CHI RODRIGUEZ

Heroes are made in moments of crisis.
CHI-CHI RODRIGUEZ

Why did the world have to grow-up?
O God how I hate the 20th Century.
PATTON

Criticism is the poison between generations.
JAMES BALDWIN

When you're a success, if you believe it, you're finished.
JAMES BALDWIN

They are lazy, rebellious,
& speak disrespectfully to their elders.
SOCRATES - 500 B.C. - THE YOUTH OF GREECE

The best life is one that faces the truth about things
squarely and harbors no illusions.
SANTAYANA

The human spirit is stronger
than anything that can happen to it.
CLAUDE LEWIS

Each generation must face its destiny.
F. D. ROOSEVELT

When you talk, you repeat what you already know;
when you listen, you often learn something.
JARED SPARKS

He who defends everything defends nothing.
FREDERICK THE GREAT

Please everybody, nobody's pleased;
please yourself at least you're pleased.
V. P. COLLINS

Let no man possess what belongs to every man.
HUGO GROTIUS - THE SEA

Impossible things are happening everyday.
OSCAR HAMMERSTEIN'S "CINDERELLA"

Nothing in life is to be feared; it is only to be understood.
MARIE CURIE

One never realizes how much and how little he knows until he starts talking.
LOUIS L'AMOUR

We must live together as brothers and sisters or perish together as fools.
MARTIN LUTHER KING

None are so empty as those who are full of themselves.
BEN WHICHCOTE

Smooth seas do not make skillful sailors.
AFRICAN PROVERB

We must all hang together or surely we shall all hang separately.
BEN FRANKLIN

The first great Commandment is:
Don't let them scare you.
ELMER DAVIS

I never heard of a Tiger becoming a vegetarian.
PANAMANIAN REVOLUTIONARY

My mind is young, but my body is dying.
NAPOLEON

Nothing makes people age faster than fear.
DEEPAK CHOPRA

The mind replenishes itself in silence.
DEEPAK CHOPRA

A half truth is a whole lie.
YIDDISH PROVERB

In the constant battle between the stream and the rock,
the stream will win with perseverance.
ANON.

Any simple problem can be made insoluble,
if enough meetings are held to discuss it.
ANON.

Winning for yourself is empty,
winning for your teammates is great.
RONNIE LOTT

Nothing great is ever accomplished without great
enthusiasm.
RALPH WALDO EMERSON

If the blind lead the blind,
both shall fall into the ditch.
ST. MATTHEW

When elephants fight, it is the grass that suffers.
KIKUYU PROVERB

We must either find a way or make one.
HANNIBAL

Selfishness is the only real atheism.
ISRAEL ZANGWINK

Success has ruined many a man.
BEN FRANKLIN

The crisis of yesterday is the joke of tomorrow.
H. G. WELLS

You only fail if you stop trying.
ANON.

Of all things valuable the greatest are
independence and freedom.
HO CHI MINH

Only Grandmothers should be allowed to start wars.
JOHN QUINN

When you win, nothing hurts.
JOE NAMATH

You can get just as drunk on your emotions
as you can on liquor!!
JOHN CHANEY

Every generation imagines itself to be more intelligent
than the one that went before it
and wiser than the one that comes after it.
GEORGE CONWELL

The ruin of a nation begins in the home of its people.
AFRICAN PROVERB

In Washington only the statues are incorruptible.
MICHAEL BOWEN

Common sense must be the most equitably shared thing
in the world because every man
is convinced he is well supplied with it.
DESCARTES

God hated the common man because he made him so
common.
OSCAR WILDE

Motivation is what gets you started.
Habit is what keeps you going.
JIM RYAN - OLYMPIC RUNNER

If a man's word wasn't any good,
it wasn't made any better by writing it down.
H. S. TRUMAN

He who becomes obsessed with a puzzle
is not very likely to solve it.
CYRIL CONNOLLY

A man can be destroyed but not defeated.
HEMINGWAY

Eighty percent of success is just showing up.
WOODY ALLEN

It's not that I'm afraid to die, it's just that
I don't want to be there when it happens.
WOODY ALLEN

Fear is lack of knowledge.
TIM LYNCH

It is better to be prepared without an opportunity,
than to have an opportunity and not be prepared.
LES BROWN

If you tell the truth you don't have to remember
anything.
BILL LYON

The trained will is a masterful weapon.
ROBERTO ASSAGIOLI

People who do not love you, make you laugh.
People who do love you make you cry.
ITALIAN PROVERB

No coach ever won a game by what he knows,
its what his players have learned.
AMOS ALONZO STAGG

They mowed our children down like blades of grass.
PEASANT - SERBIAN WOMAN

We now have authors who have written
more books than they have read.
ANON.

Wealth, power and prestige,
you can acquire all you want and still feel empty.
LEE ATWATER

Television steals far more from our lives than it brings
to them.
BILL McKIBBEN

Anger is a symptom - a way of cloaking feelings, most of
all, fear.
JOAN RIVERS

Only God is in a position to look down on anyone.
SARAH BROWN

No matter what accomplishments you achieve,
somebody helps you.
ALTHEA GIBSON

To die from smoking is to die for nothing.
AD CAMPAIGN

History doesn't repeat itself, people repeat themselves.
J. C. COOPER

For a person not to achieve the things he has an opportunity to do is such a waste of life, not for selfishness, but for what you can do for others.
JAKE SIMMONS, JR.

Adolescence is that period in life when children are certain that they will never be as dumb as their parents.
BILL LYON

Life is half spent before we know what it is.
ANON.

We come here for just a spell and then pass on, so get a few laughs and do the best you can, live your life so that whenever you lose, you are ahead.
WILL ROGERS

I didn't fail 9,000 times, I discovered 9,000 new ways which didn't work.
THOMAS EDISON

Life is being on the tightrope,
the rest is just standing around.
BOB FOSSE

Life is trouble, only in death is there peace.
ANTHONY QUINN - ZORBA

I refuse to believe in aging, rather I believe in forever altering ones aspect of the sun.
VIRGINIA WOLFE

Restricted or strict diets are dangerous, extremes must be avoided.
HIPPOCRATES 400 B.C.

Show me a hero and I'll write you a tragedy.
F.S. FITZGERALD

You can fool some of the people all of the time, all of the people some of the time, but you cannot fool all of the people, all of the time.
A. K. McCLURE

On the whole, with scandalous exceptions, democracy has given the ordinary worker more dignity than he ever had.
S. LEWIS

No race can prosper until it learns that there is as much dignity in tilling a field as in writing a poem.
B. T. WASHINGTON

If you pick up a starving dog and make him prosperous, he will not bite you. That is the principal difference between a dog and a man.
MARK TWAIN

To err is human, to forgive divine.
ALEXANDER POPE

And, departing, leave behind us footprints on the sands of time.
LONGFELLOW

An expert is one who knows more and more about less and less.
N. M. BUTLER

Nothing gives a higher return than silence.
ANON.

Nothing pays off like the restraint of tongue and pen.
ANON.

History is written by the winners.
ANON.

Happiness is an acquired art. You must practice it.
ANON.

In war, the victor only seems to win.
ANON.

Some people speak from experience.
Others, from experience, don't speak.
IRVIN S. COBB

Be wary of people who use three syl/la/ble words.
They don't know what they want to say.
SY GROSS - N.D. '58

The proper study of mankind is man.
ALEXANDER POPE

Here and there were great men who on their own changed history.
SYDNEY HOOK ON NELSON MANDELLA

Being entirely honest with one self is good exercise.
SIGMUND FREUD

Reading is to the mind, what exercise is to the body.
SIR RICHARD STEELE

I felt the only way to defend myself was to shoot back first.
JERVEY TERVALON

If you can control a nation's commerce,
it matters little which laws it passes.
BARON ROTHSCHILD

If we stand by idly while others freedoms are destroyed,
it makes each of us a coward.
ABRAHAM LINCOLN

The first impression that one gets of a ruler and of his brains is from seeing the men he has about him.
MACHIAVELLI

He who builds on the people, builds on mud, unless you have laid your foundation well.
MACHIAVELLI

Never give your love to anything that is not capable of loving you in return.
MR. "T"

The thing you've got to remember is that we've all been on scholarship since the third grade.
BILL RUSSELL - BOSTON CELTICS

Forget the fairytale that the main meaning of life is to be happy. The only true happiness is to share the sufferings of the unhappy.
YEVGENY YEVTUSHENKO - SOVIET POET

There are casualties in every war.
CECIL B. MOORE

Real change takes place - in feelings.
GEORGE WEINBERG

When the pain of being the way we are is greater than the pain of changing, we find the motivation we need.
GEORGE WEINBERG

Power is most effective when you don't have to use it,
each time you use it, you lose it a little.
J. L. CHESTNUT

It's far easier to beat a team that expects to lose
than one that came to win.
J. L. CHESTNUT

The harder you practice, the luckier you get.
GARY PLAYER - SATCHEL PAIGE

Jealousy is a wasted emotion.
GREG NORMAN

And this above all, to thine own self be true.
For then surely it must follow as the night, the day;
thou can'st do no wrong to any man.
SHAKESPEARE

I'd rather see a good sermon than hear one.
ANON.

A recession is when you are unemployed;
a depression is when I am unemployed.
ANON.

Nothing is so strong as gentleness;
Nothing is so gentle as real strength.
ST. FRANCIS DE SALES

The players are a reflection of their coach.
BILL LYON

It's what you learn after you know it all that counts.
JOHN WOODEN

You've got to be in position for luck to happen.
Luck doesn't go around looking for a stumblebum.
DARREL ROYAL

All men should strive to learn before they die
what they are running from, and to, and why.
JAMES THURBER

Friends divide sorrow and multiply joy.
CICERO

Life is not any fun when you're on top of things.
JOHN MELLENCAMP

What the world needs is more love and less paperwork.
PEARL BAILEY

People who are always complaining are probably not
working hard enough.
JAY LENO

Things constantly change,
if we cannot adjust to change, change will strangle us.
ROBERT KENNEDY

Do your duty in all things.
You cannot do more. You should never wish to do less.
ROBERT E. LEE

It is well that war is so terrible,
or we might grow too fond of it.
ROBERT E. LEE

Strike the tent.
ROBERT E. LEE - DYING WORDS

Seize the day. - Carpe Diem.
ROMANS

Television is a device that permits people who haven't
anything to do, to watch people who can't do anything.
FRED ALLEN

If you don't blow your own horn,
the world will use it as a spittoon.
G. CARLE

I always do my best,
someone might be seeing me for their first and only
time. I want them to remember me at my best.
JOE DiMAGGIO

I have been driven many times to my knees by the
overwhelming conviction that I had nowhere else to go.
ABRAHAM LINCOLN

Whenever I complain, it makes the devil smile.
ETHEL WATERS

You learn to say "no" to yourself,
before you try to make somebody else say "yes" to you.
ANON.

Those who are too smart to engage in politics are
punished by being governed by those who are dumber.
PLATO

Your reputation is what people say about you
behind your back.

Those with the worst tempers
are those who know their wrong.
ANON.

The poor need more money, the rich say the same thing.
All we want is a little more than we'll ever get.

What will we do if all our problems aren't solved by the
time we die?
BILL LYON

It's not the mountain that defeats most people,
it's the little pebble in their shoe.
CLAUDE LEWIS

If you can dream it; you can do it.
WALT DISNEY

I use hate as a weapon to defend myself; had I been
strong, I would have never needed that kind of weapon.
Hell is in an empty heart.
Do not be merciful, but be just.

Life is desire and determination.
There may be virtue in sin.
KAHLIL GIBRAN

If you are patient in one moment of anger,
you will escape a hundred days of sorrow.
CHINESE PROVERB

What lies behind and what lies ahead of us is of little
importance when compared to what lies within.
OLIVER W. HOLMES

Whoever is happy will make others happy, too.
ANNE FRANK

Our nature consists in motion; complete rest is death.
BLAISE PASCAL

Don't soak the rich,
soak the poor.
There's more of them.
ERIC WRIGHT

As a man, I think you a scoundrel,
but as a President, I salute you.
Enemy of **F. D. ROOSEVELT**

To be prepared is half the victory.
CERVANTES

When it is dark enough, men see the stars.
RALPH WALDO EMERSON

Losing when you're not doing your best
teaches you nothing.
BUD WILKINSON

I can make a thousand Lords but not one daVinci.
FRANCIS I, KING OF ITALY

Golf is played on a 5 1/2" course,
the space between the ears.
BOBBY JONES

Service to others is the rent I pay for my room on earth.
MUHAMMAD ALI

You never realize how small a ring can be,
until you're in it.
SUGAR RAY ROBINSON

Good loser's get into the habit of losing.
KNUTE ROCKNE

Wearing underwear is as formal
as I ever hope to get.
HEMINGWAY

He could practice abstinence, but not temperance.
JAMES BOSWELL

Most people are about as happy
as they make up their minds to be.
ABRAHAM LINCOLN

When I was in the batter's box, I felt sorry for the pitcher.
ROGER HORNSBY

I've always believed that anybody with a little ability, a little guts and the desire to apply himself can make it.
WILLIE SHOEMAKER

I use the word hungry to describe what I mean when I talk about desire. Being hungry provides you with the physical and mental energies necessary for success.
ARA PARSEGIAN

I hope that I can always desire more than I can accomplish.
MICHAELANGELO

You can't get much done in life if you work only on the days when you feel good.
JERRY WEST

Me? I loved to hit.
BABE RUTH

Fame is vapor, popularity is an accident, money takes wings. Those who cheer you today may curse you tomorrow.
LEE TREVINO

The best thing you can give another person is one more chance.
BILL LYON

If I ever get to the point where I'm playing it safe,
I'll quit.
MILES DAVIS

In the long run, greatness makes itself apparent.
AGNES DeMILLE

The fight is never over.
JACKIE ROBINSON

Winning the Super Bowl was not the biggest reward.
The work involved in getting there was.
JOE GREENE

There is no such thing as a natural.
SUGAR RAY ROBINSON

There are no secrets to success. It is the result of
preparation, hard work and learning from failures.
COLIN POWELL

You've got to learn to turn the page.
JOHN CHANEY

The secret to a happy & rewarding life is self-discipline.
PROF. EDWARD FISCHER

Laws grind the poor, and rich men rule the law.
GOLDSMITH

A little learning is a dangerous thing.
ALEXANDER POPE

A liar needs a good memory.
QUINTILIAN

Oh, wad some pow'r the giftie gi'e us
---to see oursel's as others see us!
ROBERT. BURNS

Man's love is of man's life a thing apart,
'tis woman's whole existence.
LORD BYRON

To say that you can love one person all of your life
is just like saying that one candle will continue burning
as long as you live.
TOLSTOY

Man is the only beast of prey, and indeed,
the only beast that preys on its own species.
WILLIAM JAMES

A sound mind in a sound body.
JUVENAL

No one has the right to educate.
TOLSTOY

I cannot afford to waste my time making money.
AGASSIZ

When it is a question of money,
everybody is of the same religion.
VOLTAIRE

What is moral is what made you feel good after
and what is immoral is what made you feel bad after.
HEMINGWAY

For the hand that rocks the cradle
is the hand that rules the world.
W. S. ROSS

Music hath charms to soothe a savage beast.
CONGREVE

Necessity is the mother of invention.
ANON.

When a dog bites a man that is not news, but when a
man bites a dog that is news.
J. B. BOGART OR C. A. DANA

Two men look out through the same bars:
one sees the mud, and one the stars.
LANGBRIDGE

The optimist sees the doughnut,
the pessimist, the hole.
MEL WILSON

Children begin by loving their parents;
as they grow older they judge them;
sometimes they forgive them.
OSCAR WILDE

Those who cannot remember the past
are condemned to repeat it.
SANTAYANA

No man can be a patriot on an empty stomach.
W. C. BRANN

If at first you don't succeed try, try, try again.
W. E. HICKSON

Poverty - The most deadly and prevalent of all diseases.
EUGENE O'NEILL

When the Gods wish to punish us they answer our prayers.
OSCAR WILDE

Practice what you preach.
PLATIUS

Prejudice is the child of ignorance.
W. HAZLETT

It is never too late to give up your prejudices.
THOREAU

Whilst we have prisons
it matters little which of us occupies the cells.
G. B. SHAW

The heart has reasons of which reason has no knowledge.
PASCAL

Reform must come from within, not from without, you cannot legislate virtue.
CARDINAL GIBBONS

For all sad words of tongue or pen, the saddest are these: It might have been.
J. G. WHITTIER

All religions must be tolerated--for--every man must get to Heaven his own way.
FREDERICK THE GREAT

Every revolution was first a thought in one man's mind.
RALPH WALDO EMERSON

It is better to wear out than to rust out.
RICHARD CUMBERLAND

If slavery is not wrong, nothing is wrong.
ABRAHAM LINCOLN

The man worthwhile is the one who will smile when everything goes wrong.
ELLA W. WILCOX

Why doesn't everybody leave everybody else
the hell alone.
JIMMY DURANTE

Life is too important to be taken seriously.
ANON.

I am not responsible for the first thought
that enters my mind,
the second thought is mine.
BOB LENNOX

Force, if unassisted by judgement,
collapses through its own mass.
HORACE 45 B.C.

God gets you to the plate,
but once your there your on your own.
TED WILLIAMS

Pable Casals in his 80's practiced 4-5 hours a day: ----
I have a notion I am making progress.
ANON.

I may not like what you say
but I will defend to the death your right to say it.
CHARDIN

The guy who complains about the way the ball bounces is likely the one who dropped it.
LOU HOLTZ

It became necessary to destroy the village to save it.
FIELD OFFICER - VIETNAM

Success is inspiration, aspiration and perspiration.
CLAUDE LEWIS

The dreamers are the saviors of the world.
JAMES ALLEN

Doubt and fear are the great enemies of knowledge.
JAMES ALLEN

If you stick to one thing, you not only date yourself, but you also dwarf your mind.
RALPH COOPER

We are what we read.
GEORGE WILL

Let thy food, be thy medicine.
THOMAS EDISON

Sooner or later, talent always gets equalized.
JOHN CHANEY

Celebrities are people with great big holes in themselves.
JULIA PHILLIPS

When you underestimate an opponent,
it's the beginning of your demise.
ANDRE McCARTER

There are those who make things happen,
there are those who watch things happen,
and those who wonder what happened.
ANON.

A Goal is a dream with a deadline.
ANON.

If it weren't for the last minute,
nothing would get done.
ANON.

Silence is the ultimate weapon of power.
DeGAULLE

Better shoeless, than bookless.
ICELANDIC PROVERB

Teachers are taught by their pupils.
OSCAR HAMMERSTIEN

An angry person is not a successful person.
HANK AARON

A man may lose many times,
but he isn't a loser until he starts to
blame someone else.
ANON.

The strongest of all warriors are these two;
time & patience.
TOLSTOY

Fear will not harm you, but the fear of failure will.
ANON.

You want to make God laugh, tell him your plans.
ANON.

Through discipline one achieves.
ANON.

It's a proven fact - bumble bees cannot fly,
it is physically and scientifically impossible,
it's just that no-one told the bumblebees.
ANON.

I want to go out like a man, instead of a bottle cap.
CURT FLOOD

Everyone is a genius at least once a year.
G. C. LICHTENBURG

What you are, off; you are on.
PETER O'TOOLE

Obstacles are things a person sees when he takes his
eyes off his goals.
E. JOSEPH COSSMAN

Man never made any material as resilient
as the human spirit.
JASON WILLIAMS

The moment of victory is much too short to live for that
and nothing else.
MARTINA NAVRATILOVA

The only man who never makes a mistake
is the man who never does anything.
TEDDY ROOSEVELT

Life is like riding a bicycle, you don't fall off
unless you stop pedaling.
CLAUDE PEPPER

A loving heart is the truest wisdom.
CHARLES DICKENS

Success has a simple formula;
do your best and people may like it.
SAM EWING

The hardest thing in life to learn is
which bridge to cross and which to burn.
DAVID RUSSELL

A professional is someone who can
do his best work when he doesn't feel like it.
ALLISTAR COOKE

A little knowledge that acts is worth infinitely
more than much knowledge that is idle.
GIBSON

One just man causes the devil greater affliction
than a million blind believers.
KAHLIL GIBRAN

In the midst of winter,
I found within me an invincible summer.
ALBERT CAMUS

Men often act unlike themselves.
TOLSTOY

A man should keep his friendships in constant repair.
SAMUEL JOHNSON

You can make all A's in school
and go out and flunk life.
WALKER PERCY

It is the journey, not the destination, that matters.
JOSEPH EPSTEIN

It often requires more bravery to tell the simple truth
than it does to win a battle.
JOSH BILLINGS

No pleasure is comparable to the standing upon the
vantage ground of truth.
FRANCES BACON

Never seem wiser, nor more learned,
than the people you are with.
LORD CHESTERFIELD

Revenge is a confession of pain.
SENECA

The world is a looking glass, and gives back to every
man the reflection of his own face.
WILLIAM THACKERAY

There is only one religion,
though there are a hundred versions of it.
G.B. SHAW

Those who say it can't be done, should stay out of the
way of those who are doing it.
ANON.

I think the key to success in life is the people we choose to associate with, who we choose as our friends.
WILT CHAMBERLAIN

The human body is designed to fix itself.
DR. WARREN LEVINE

A team that cannot concentrate, cannot win.
JOE PATERNO

Deep down, all athletes yearn for discipline.
CHARLIE PITMAN - PENN STATE

Success is getting up just one more time than you fall down.
GENE COTTON

If you're filled with pride, you wont have any room for wisdom.
RALPH WALDO EMERSON

Words can't break bones, but they can break hearts.
RALPH WALDO EMERSON

Do the things you fear - and the death of fear is certain.
RALPH WALDO EMERSON

You can't stay mad at somebody who makes you laugh.
JAY LENO

We are made to persist.
That's how we find out who we are.
THOMAS WOLFE

You can have it all, you just can't have it all at once.
OPRAH WINFREY

The minute you settle for less than you deserve, you get even less than you settled for.
MAUREEN DOWD

All of humanities problems stem from man's inability to sit quietly in a room alone.
BLAISE PASCAL

We cannot forever hide the truth about ourselves, from ourselves.
JOHN MC CAIN

Everything becomes a little different as soon as it is spoken out loud.
HERMANN HESSE

They say money is the root of all evil, but I'll take money over being broke any old day of the week.
MAE WEST

Bet on the toss of a coin that God is. If we win, we win eternity. If we lose, we lose nothing.
BLAISE PASCAL

Things that bother you are trying to teach you something.
ANON.

The right kind of fear prompts us to do right.
ANON.

The Chinese have the same character for success and failure.
ANON.

The purpose of education is to make the young as unlike their elders as possible.
WOODROW WILSON

We jail little thieves and take our hats off to great ones.
ANON.

The biggest burden - potential.
ANON.

Whatever needs to be maintained through force is doomed.
HENRY MILLER

Age does not protect you from love, but love, to some extent, protects you from age.
JEANNE MOREAU

The humiliation you feel after doing something stupid;
The elation when you realize, no one else saw it.
ANON.

I will permit no man to narrow and degrade my soul
by making me hate him.
B.T. WASHINGTON

The soul would have no rainbow had the eyes no tears.
JOHN VANCE CHENEY

When you try hard, you never fail;
the only failure is failing to try.
GERT JOHNSON

Victory is certain if we have the courage to believe and
the strength to run your own race.
GERT JOHNSON

Success is much more difficult to live with than failure.
ANON.

If you want the rainbow,
you have to put up with the rain.
ANON.

If your ship doesn't come in, swim out to it.
ANON.

You can't get rid of poverty by giving people money.
J. O'ROURKE

Only a fool tests the depth of the water with both feet.
AFRICAN PROVERB

You're worst humiliation is only someone else's momentary entertainment.
KAREN CROCKETT

From what we get, we can make a living; what we give however, makes a life.
ARTHUR ASHE

Every man thinks God is on his side; the rich and powerful know he is.
JEAN ANOUILN

Today is a great triumph over yesterday's tragedies.

Today is only the tomorrow that you dreaded yesterday.

You can look at life in two ways: One, that there is no such thing as a miracle. Two, that everything is a miracle.
EINSTEIN

Act as if you were already happy
and that will tend to make you happy.
DALE CARNEGIE

Life begets life; energy creates energy. It is by spending
oneself that one becomes rich.
SARAH BERNHARDT

Don't give in! Make your own trail.
KATHERINE HEPBURN

You may have to fight a battle more than once to win it.
MARGARET THATCHER

Life is like a ten speed bike. Most of us have gears we
never use.
CHARLES SHULTZ

A pessimist never won a battle.
DWIGHT D. EISENHOWER

It was the initiative and the intuitiveness
of the average G. I. that won the war.
DWIGHT D. EISENHOWER

Sport is a way of proving you are better than somebody
else at something that's of no use to anybody.
NOEL CARROLL

Any day that I am not being physically tortured
is a great day.
MERRILL MARKOE

You'd better love living, because dying is a real
pain in the ass.
FRANK SINATRA

I asked for all things that I might enjoy life, instead I
was given life that I might enjoy all things.
PARADOX

Success is failure turned inside out.
FROM "DON'T QUIT"

He who pretends to look on death without fear lies.
ROUSSEAU

The hour of death has arrived, and we go our ways - I
to die, and you to live. Which is better God only knows.
SOCRATES

Exercise is king, nutrition is queen.

What you eat today, you are tomorrow.

If you eat junk today, your body feels like junk
tomorrow, eat junk everyday and your body becomes
junk.
JACK LA LANE

Love isn't blind, it sees more, not less. But because it sees more, it is willing to see less.

Nothing is interesting if you're not interested.

Convert stumbling blocks into stepping stones.
BEN FRANKLIN

To be completely satisfied with yourself
is a sure sign that progress is about to end.

The only absolute mistake is the one from which we learn nothing.

Having two ears and only one tongue, we should probably listen twice as much as we speak.

A diamond is a chunk of coal made good under pressure.

If you wait for perfect conditions you'll never get anything done.
BEN FRANKLIN

Let our advance worrying
become our advance thinking and planning.
WINSTON CHURCHILL

A man dies once, a coward ten thousand times.
ANON.

Practice each minute as if it will be your last; It will help you to give your best.
ANON.

When the boredom becomes fun, you win.
ANON.

I sought my soul, but my soul I could not see. I sought my god, but my god eluded me. I sought my brother and found all three.
ANON.

The best thing about saying nothing is the fact that it cannot be repeated.
ANON.

Sooner or later, we all sleep alone.
JOAN RIVERS

We are often troubled, but not crushed; sometimes in doubt, but never in despair; there are many enemies, but we are never without a friend.
ST. PAUL

The greatest of all faults is to be conscious of none.
THOMAS CARLYLE

Do not let what you cannot do interfere with what you can do.
JOHN WOODEN

When they come to throw me on the scrap heap,
I want to go fighting and clawing every inch of the way.
G.B. SHAW

If people are good enough for God,
then they are good enough for me.

Listening is a form of talking.

We are what we do.
MATT TALBOT

Doctors pour drugs of which they know little, to cure
diseases, of which they know less, into human beings of
whom they know nothing.
VOLTAIRE

It ain't bragging if you can back it up.
DIZZY DEAN

There are no great deeds,
only small deeds and great love.
MOTHER THERESA

Every hero becomes a bore at last.
RALPH WALDO EMERSON

Always give 100%
and you'll never have to second guess yourself.
TOMMY JOHN

There is only one good, knowledge,
and one evil, ignorance.
SOCRATES

Every artist was first an amateur.
EMERSON

Silence can never be misquoted.
BOB MONKHOUSE

You are never sorry for your kindnesses.
PROCHNOW

War is the inevitable outcome of bad politics.
CLAUSEWITS

Fear without respect is nothing.
JOE HICKS

The joy of giving is much greater than the joy of
receiving.
HAROLD REYNOLDS

You are only as good as the other fellow thinks you are,
and you're only as bad as you allow yourself to think
you are.
JAMES CAGNEY

Young blood must have its course
lad, and every dog his day.
KINGSLEY

The true university is a collection of books.
CARLYLE

We must remember virtue is not hereditary.
PAYNE

Everything comes to those who can wait.
RABELIAS

Man wants but little here below,
nor wants that little long.
GOLDSMITH

My belief is that to have no wants is divine.
SOCRATES

Resistance to tyrants is obedience to God.
THOMAS JEFFERSON

Truth is the most valuable thing we have.
MARK TWAIN

A truth that's told with bad intent beats
all the lies you can invent.
BLAKE

If you have nothing to say, be quiet.
ANON.

When you find yourself in the hole, stop digging.
GEORGE WILL

When you think you know baseball, you don't.
YOGI BERRA

Money is the root of all evil, but it buys stuff.
ANON.

When people say "It's not the money", it's the money.
E.R. MURROW

When we have not what we like,
we must like what we have.
BUBSY - RABUTIN

Our country, right or wrong.
STEPHEN DECATUR

O death! The poor man's dearest friend -
the kindest and the best.
ROBERT BURNS

There are two tragedies in life,
one is not to get your heart's desire.
The other is to get it.
G.B. SHAW

Let no man write my epitaph.
ROBERT EMMET

Experience is a dear school,
yet fools will learn in no other.
BEN FRANKLIN

Doing easily what other's find difficult is a talent; doing
what is impossible for talent is genius.
AMIEL

The Golden Rule is that there is no Golden Rule.
G.B. SHAW

The will to win is not nearly as important
as the will to prepare to win.
BOBBY KNIGHT

What you can do, or dream you can, begin it.
Boldness has genius, power and magic in it.
GOETHE

Creative genius is very close to insanity.
PATRICIA MARX

The chickens are coming home to roost.
MALCOLM X

The greatest tragedy is not to love and lose,
but to leave this world without knowing love at all.
ISABELLE ALLONDE

You use the school, don't let the school use you.
MARK MACON

All warfare is based on deception.
SUN TZU

The ability to gain victory by changing and adapting
according to the opponent is called genius.
SUN TZU

Even a broken clock is right twice a day.
ANON.

They are lazy, superstitious, dishonest slum dwellers
with a propensity for violence.
1850 NEWSPAPER EDITORIAL "IRISH"

Sports serve society by providing examples of
excellence.
GEORGE WILL

Those hectic times we live in will someday be the
"Good Old Days" for our children.
GLADYS KNIGHT

People don't plan to fail,
they fail because they don't plan.
ANON.

It's hard to write for people that need you. It's easy to
write for people that don't need you.
ANDY ROONEY

I calls 'em like I see 'em.
TOM GORMAN--UMPIRE

I calls 'em the way they are.
ALBERT EINSTEIN

The theory of the "Old One" (GOD)

He (GOD) is not playing at dice.
ALBERT EINSTEIN

If you see dirt on top of the rug,
there's a lot more dirt underneath.
JOHN CHANEY

Nothing motivates like your own failure.
BO SCHEMBECHLER

If a man says it is completely clear, he does not really
understand the subject.
NIELS BOHR

Hatred is a negative force.
SIMON ESTES

I'd like to think that each of us can become a quality person who's having a bad day, rather than an inferior person who's having a good day.
DARRELL SIFFORD

If we do something often enough, the sting goes out of it, and before long, we're not afraid of it anymore.
GEORGE WEINBERG

There is no loneliness greater than the loneliness of failure.
ERIC HOFFER

Life is like acting. It takes a lot of rehearsals for a man to learn to be himself.
JAMES CAGNEY

We are all born into the world with nothing. Everything we acquire after that is profit.
SAM EWING

Why get all worked up over something that never was? Some things are worth your anger and some aren't.
BARNEY EWELL - OLYMPIC RUNNER

Success isn't going to chase you. You have to go after it.
ANON.

There is only one way to coast, and that is downhill.
PAUL BROWN

Any day above ground is a good day.
GENE SIMMONS

There are many things in life that will catch your eye.
But only a few things that will catch your heart.
Pursue those.
PHIL MARTELLI

You can't eat sympathy.
ALLEN HEATH

If you want to know what people are really saying,
listen to their eyes.
BILL LYON

I don't think it's very dignified to be in a rock band at
all. I mean, I just hope people don't laugh
when we get out there.
MICK JAGGER

The more success you have, the more responsibility you
have for giving something back.
SONNY HILL

Don't put people on pedestals,
they can break falling down or up.
ANON.

I never get nervous, if you have talent you get nervous.
I never get nervous.
GEORGE BURNS

Losers are winners who don't realize they are yet.
TONY ROBBINS

One machine can do the work of fifty ordinary men.
Fifty machines cannot do the work of one extraordinary man.
L. RON HUBBARD

Having the courage to admit defeat sometimes
can be a victory.
BILL LYON

From each according to his ability,
to each according to his need.
KARL MARX

All government without the consent of the governed
is the very essence of slavery.
JONATHAN SWIFT

Defeat may serve as well as victory.
ED MARKHAM

Most men perish, inch by inch, who play at little games.
ANON.

A good part of what people consider aging
is not aging at all - it's disuse.
HERBERT DE VRIES

To the victor belong the spoils.
M. MARCY

There is but one step from sublime to the ridiculous.
NAPOLEON

He who can, does. He who cannot, teaches.
G.B. SHAW

When everybody thinks the same, nobody thinks.
BILL WALTON

I never heard a dying man say: "My only regret is that I
didn't spend more time at the office".
ANON.

It's a funny thing about life: If you refuse to accept
anything but the very best, you will often get it.
SOMERSET MAUGHAN

The only limit to our realization of tomorrow
will be our doubts of today.
F.D.R.

People only lose after they give up hope.
CLAUDE LEWIS

There is not a fiercer hell then the failure
of great object.
KEATS

When someone dies, regret not that you never had a
chance to say goodbye, but regret deeply if you never
took the time to say hello.
MICHAEL SMYTH WALLINGFORD

I don't regret the things I've done, I only regret the
things I wanted to do and didn't.
INGRID BERGMAN

Avoid having your ego so close to your position,
that when your position falls, your ego goes with it.
COLIN POWELL

Let us be servants in order to be leaders.
DOSTOYEVSKY

The main ingredient of stardom is the rest of the team.
There is no replacement for sound fundamentals
and strict discipline.
Learn as if you were to live forever;
live as if you were to die tomorrow.
The true athlete should have character,
not be a character.
Talent is God-given; be humble. Fame is man - given;
be thankful. Conceit is self-given; be careful.
JOHN WOODEN

Hell is not to love anymore.
GEORGES BERNANOS

Intensified progress seems to be bound
with intensified unfreedom.
MARCOSE

A single grateful thought towards heaven is the most
complete prayer.
LESSING

No man ever prayed heartily without learning
something.
RALPH WALDO EMERSON

Words don't move mountains. Work, exacting work,
moves mountains.
DANILO DOLCI

Angels can fly because they take themselves lightly.
G.K. CHESTERTON

If you're right, why argue. If you're wrong, why argue.
Either way, you prove nothing.
ANON.

What you cannot enforce, do not command.
SOPHOCLES

I have never heard a successful person say:
"I owe everything to drugs and alcohol".
LOU HOLTZ

Fatigue will eventually make cowards of us all.
VINCE LOMBARDI

Sometimes the holes we dig for other people turn out to
be our own graves.
BEVERLY WILLIAMS

Today is always temporary.
ELLEN GOODMAN

Growing old ain't for sissies.
BETTE DAVIS

A good solution may become your next problem.

We fear the things we want the most.

Feelings of inferiority and superiority both come from fear.

The biggest risk in life is not risking.

Excuses are a lack of faith in your own power.

To get what you want, help other people get what they want.

If you prepare for old age, old age comes sooner.

In giving a gift, note your true intentions.

Be natural - not normal.

Worry comes from the belief that you are powerless.

If you are afraid to lose something, at some point you will lose it.

If you have to be happy, you will always be unhappy.
DR. ROBERT ANTHONY

Nothing signals mediocrity like
the excessive awarding of prizes.
MELVIN MADDOCKS

The liars punishment is not in the least that he is not
believed, but that he cannot believe anyone else.
G.B. SHAW

The talent of success is nothing more than doing what
you can do well, and doing well whatever you do.
LONGFELLOW

The only thing necessary for evil to prevail
is for good men to do nothing.
ANON.

If you have class, you don't need much of anything else.
If you don't have it, no matter what else you have,
it doesn't make much difference.
WILLIE MAYS

The line between hunger and anger is a thin line.
JOHN STEINBECK

Imitation is the sincerest form of flattery.
C. COLTON

The strongest man in the world
is he who stands most alone.
IBSEN

God will not look you over for medals,
degrees or diplomas, but for scars.
L. RON HUBBARD

Facts are the enemy of truth.
CERVANTES

Only he who attempts the absurd is capable of
achieving the impossible.
CERVANTES

Freedom is never made stronger by denying basic rights
to those whose views are divergent from our own.
CLAUDE LEWIS

Long range goals keep you from being frustrated
by short range failures.
CHAS. C. NOBLE

This thing called "failure" is not the falling down,
but the staying down.
MARY PICKFORD

Failures are never final.
ANON.

Don't analyze life, live it.
HUGH PRATHER

Whenever I find myself arguing for something with great passion, I can be certain I'm not convinced.
HUGH PRATHER

Things do not change, we change.
THOREAU

Character is what you are in the dark.
DWIGHT L. MOODY

'Tis better to be alone than in bad company.
GEORGE WASHINGTON

Conscience is God's presence in man.
SWEDENBORG

Any job is a self - portrait of the person doing it.
ANON.

Destiny is not a matter of chance, but of choice. It is not something given, but to be attained.
W.J. BRYAN - BART STARR

As we grow older, memories become the cushions of life.
GARY PLAYER

Any fool can make a rule and every fool will follow it.
THOREAU

Hating people is like burning down your own house to get rid of a rat.
R. FOSDICK

The heart of a fool is in his mouth, but the mouth of a wise man is in his heart.
BEN FRANKLIN

What is history but a fable agreed upon?
NAPOLEON BONAPARTE

An honest man is the noblest work of God.
ROBERT BURNS

There is no king who has not had a slave among his ancestors, and no slave who has not had a king among his.
HELEN KELLER

Knowledge is power.
HOBBES

He laughs best that laughs last.
VAN BURGH

Man is the only animal that blushes, or needs to.
MARK TWAIN

Morality is a private and costly luxury.
HENRY ADAMS

We have just enough religion to make us hate, but not enough to make us love, one another.
JONATHAN SWIFT

When dreams come true they may turn into a nightmare.

Even a lie tells some truth about the person who tells it.

Pious verbiage can be a camouflage for venom.

Those that lack the capacity to achieve much in an atmosphere of freedom will clamor for power.
ERIC HOFFER

Religion makes life meaningful, by complicating.

The purpose of a philosopher is to show people what is right under their noses.

No one has the right to happiness.

A man's heart is a grave long before he is buried.

The true opposites: Freedom and absolute power.

To be fully alive is to feel that everything is possible.
ERIC HOFFER

He who has conquered doubt and fear
has conquered failure.
JAMES ALLEN

Thoughts of doubt and fear never accomplish anything.
JAMES ALLEN

To be a success I knew all that I needed by the time I finished Kindergarten.
ROBERT FULGHAM

Who said "Life is supposed to be fair"?
DOUG WILLIAMS

Men never do evil so completely and cheerfully as when
they do it from religious conviction.
BLAISE PASCAL

Every time we open our mouths it is because of vanity.
SPINOZA

The secret of man's being is not only to live,
but to have something to live for.
FYODOR DOSTOYEVSKY

Everything is changing. People are taking the
comedians seriously, and the politicians as a joke.
WILL ROGERS

People need responsibility. They resist assuming it, but
they cannot get along without it.
JOHN STEINBECK

Spring is when you feel like whistling
even with a shoe full of slush.
DOUG LARSON

If you want to truly understand something,
try to change it.
KURT LEWIN

Be patient with everyone, but above all, with yourself.
ST. FRANCIS DE SALES

When you aim for perfection,
you discover it's a moving target.
GEORGE FISCHER

A person all wrapped up in himself
generally makes a pretty small package.
JOS. COSSMAN

I consider it a privilege
to have been allowed to grow old.
MARY MORRISON

Success is never final.
WINSTON CHURCHILL

Between two evils, I always pick the one
I've never tried before.
MAE WEST

The graveyards are full of indispensable men.
De GAULLE

One man with courage makes a majority.
ANDREW JACKSON

The worst prison would be a closed heart.
JOHN PAUL II

For peace of mind,
resign as general manager of the universe.
LARRY EISENBERG

Nothing makes a woman more beautiful
than the belief she is beautiful.
SOPHIA LOREN

Men will lie on their backs, talking about the fall of
man, and never make an effort to get up.
THOREAU

Beware of false knowledge,
it is more dangerous than ignorance.
G.B. SHAW

Self - pity never hits a moving target.
ANON.

To succeed: The humility to prepare; the
confidence to perform.
LAURENCE OLIVIER

A football coach, you have to be smart enough to know
the game, but dumb enough to think it's important.
EUGENE McCARTHY

People have one thing in common: they are all different.
ROBERT ZEND

Even if you are on the right track,
you will get run over if you just sit there.
WILL ROGERS

Worry is the most unproductive of all human emotions.
ANON.

Most of the things we fear shall never pass.
ANON.

Don't bother other's problems.
ANON.

I believe a person can accomplish anything provided he doesn't care who receives credit.
ANON.

Deep faith eliminates fear.
LECH WALESA

You don't stop laughing because you grow old.
You grow old because you stop laughing.
MICHAEL PRITCHARD

Confidence is contagious, so is lack of confidence.
VINCE LOMBARDI

We must value the only champion we will have from birth to death - ourselves.
EDA LE SHAN

If it came cheap - our happiness and freedom - it wouldn't be worth having.
RICK BASS

"THE WAY OF LIFE"...LAO TZU

The way to do is to be.

Men's conduct should depend on their instinct and conscience.

All of life grows at one's own doorstep.

The core and surface are essentially the same.

If you never assume importance, you never lose it.

Good government comes of itself.

Man at his best, like water, serves as he goes along.

Surrounded by treasure you lie ill at ease, proud beyond measure you come to your knees.

If you can lead men without their knowing, you are at the core of life.

CONTINUATION "WAY OF LIFE"...LAO TZU

One who knows his lot to be the lot of all other men is a safe man to guide them.

One who recognizes all men as members of his own body is a sound man to guard them.

Those who flow as life flows know they need no other force.

A leader is best when people barely know that he exists.

Fail to honor people, they fail to honor you.

Pride has never brought a man greatness.

In war, conduct your triumph as a funeral.

Ambition wanders blind.

False teachers of life use flowery words and start nonsense.

Who tries to live by force shall die thereby of course.

I feel the heartbeats of others above my own.

Be concerned not with obedience but with benefit.

Those who know, do not tell, those who tell, do not know.
LAO TZU - "THE WAY OF LIFE"

Law after law breeds a multitude of thieves.

The less a leader does and says the happier his people.

The biggest problem in the world could have been solved when it was small.

If you say yes too quickly you may have to say no.

Most people who miss after almost winning, should have known the end from the beginning.

People never tire of anyone who is not bent upon comparison.

Care, be fair, be humble. When a man cares, he is unafraid, when he is fair he leaves enough for others, when he is humble, he can grow.

The greatest victor wins without a battle.

He who overcomes men understands them.

A man who knows how little he knows is well, a man who knows how much he knows is sick.

A man with outward courage dares to die, a man with inward courage dares to live.

Men who have to fight for their living are not afraid to die for it.

Though heaven prefer no man, a sensible man prefers heaven.

True living would take from those with too much enough for those with too little, whereas man extracts from those with too little still more for those with too much.

To accept destiny is to face life with open eyes.

Yield and you need not break.

Goodness comes free.

Only pursue an offender to show him the way.

The common people love a sound man because he does not talk above their level.

LAO TZU - "THE WAY OF LIFE"

Mistakes are part of the dues one pays
for a full life.
SOPHIA LOREN

Courage is very important. Like a muscle, it is
strengthened by use.
RUTH GORDON

If you think you can, you can.
And if you think you can't, you're right.
MARY KAY ASH

Money doesn't talk, money screams.

You can't get much done by starting tomorrow.

Kindness is the ability to love people more than they
deserve.

Practice makes perfect, so be careful what you practice.

You can't just turn back the clock, but you can wind it
up again.

My critics are my best friends.
OSCAR WILDE

An optimist sees opportunity in every difficulty, A
pessimist sees difficulty in every opportunity.
WINSTON CHURCHILL

There is opportunity in every difficulty.
ALBERT EINSTEIN

A lie can travel halfway around the world, while the truth is putting on its shoes.
ANON.

The life which is unexamined is not worth living.
PLATO

It is past time to go when you start asking yourself if it's time to go.
WILLIAM ROTSLER

Never ruin an apology with an excuse.
KIMBERLY JOHNSON

When tears are exhausted, laughter takes over.
WANG MENG

You have to celebrate life, not brood about death.
VIRGINIA KELLEY

Done right, life leaves stains.
VIRGINIA KELLEY

God gave us memory
so that we might have roses in December.
SIR JAMES BARRIE

I knew I would be famous some day, not because I was talented, and not because I was especially beautiful, but because I wanted it.
MARILYN MONROE

Democracy cannot be a successful general practice unless it is a true first conviction.
HERRYMON MAURER

Common sense is the self-evident principle beneath all belief.
THOMAS REID

The truth lies beneath the surface of the facts.
DR. RICHARD SELZER

The greatest person is the one who has the ability to make everyone feel great.
G.K. CHESTERTON

I never saw a Brink's truck following the Hearse.
FRANK L. RIZZO

It is better to die on one's feet than to live on ones knees.
ZAPATA

Too much of a good thing is great.
MAE WEST

God answers all prayers. But sometimes, the answer is no.
GARRY MADDOX

The people who know you best, will eventually find you out for who you really are.
ANON.

When you leave this world, the only things you take
with you are the things you give away.
ANON.

Every child is born an artist.
PICASSO

Bad news travels fast. Good news takes the scenic
route.
SARAH VAUGHAN

What you are afraid to do is a clear indicator of the next
thing you need to do.

Less effort creates more results.

You are the only teacher you will ever have.
ROBERT ANTHONY

All things in excess bring troubles.
PLAUTIUS

I don't have a lot of respect for talent. Talent is genetic.
It's what you do with it that counts.
MARTIN RITT

Do not go gentle in the good night. Rage, rage against
the dying of the light.
DYLAN THOMAS

The human brain uses 10X more oxygen
than the rest of your body.
ANON.

Big shots are only little shots that keep shooting.
CHRISTOPHER MORLEY

Some are born great, some become great, but most are
thrust into situations that require us to be great.
ANON.

You have to be with a child today to be in his
memory tomorrow.
STEFFEN KRAEHMER

Losing is just the dumbest thing in the world.
THERESA SHANK GRENTZ

The only way you can make people do anything is to
make it attractive and add a little humor.
ARNOLD SCHWARZENEGGER

TV--the plug in drug.
ANON.

You are either going to sacrifice now and enjoy life later
on, or you'll enjoy life now and sacrifice later on.
BOB SHANNON

If you rest, you rust.
HELEN HAYES

Go it old girl, you've done it well.
HELEN HAYES

Freedom's just another word for nothing else to lose.
BOB DYLAN

The race will be won or lost in your lane.
CARL LEWIS

Confidence is purely a byproduct of preparation.
PAT RILEY

When we speak, we show what we are.
GREEK PROVERB

If you are wealthy, intelligent, talented and handsome,
it is almost impossible to succeed.
GREEK PROVERB

In time of war, the law is silent.

A page in History is worth a volume of Philosophy.

Success can be a curse.
LINDA HAMILTON

Enjoy everything you can brother,
because once your dead life ain't worth living.
NAT "KING" COLE

Have the courage to face a difficult task lest it kick you
harder than you bargain for.
STANISLAUS I

I'm throwing twice as hard as I ever did,
but it's only getting there half as fast.
LEFTY GOMEZ

The only way to prove your a good sport is to lose.
ERNIE BANKS

Ninety feet between the bases is the nearest thing to
perfection that man has yet achieved.
RED SMITH

If a tie is like kissing your sister, losing is like kissing
your grandmother with her teeth out.
GEORGE BRETT

You gotta be a man to play baseball, but you gotta have
a lot of little boy in you too.
ROY CAMPANELLA

See everything. Overlook a great deal. Improve a little.
POPE JOHN XXIII

Lord, we ain't what we wanna be, we ain't what we oughta be. But thank God, we ain't what we was.
CLAUDE LEWIS

Honest arrogance or hypocritical humility.
FRANK LLOYD WRIGHT

Never hate your enemies. It clouds your thinking.
MICHAEL CORLEONE

Never let anyone know what you are thinking, it gives them an advantage.
MICHAEL CORLEONE

America and Democracy is the last, best hope on Earth.
ABRAHAM LINCOLN

Public Relations is the substitution of words for performance.
S. HERMAN

When all is said and done, the only people who stick with you through it all, is your family.
JIMMY CONNORS

The only way to make a man trustworthy is to trust him.
HENRY L. STINSON

To play yourself, to be truly able to be yourself,
is the hardest thing to do.
CARY GRANT

Everybody wants to be Cary Grant.
Even I want to be Cary Grant.
CARY GRANT

The penalty for success is to be bored
by the people who use to snub you.
NANCY ASTOR

Television has raised writing to a new low.
SAM GOLDWYN

Stupidity is the basic building block of the universe.
FRANK ZAPPA

The trouble with the world is that the stupid are sure
and the intelligent are full of doubt.
BETRAND RUSSELL

Television - the moronic national baby-sitter.
ROBERT HUGHES

To me indifference is the epitome of evil.
ELI WIESEL

Success has ruined many a man.
BEN FRANKLIN

The only happiness is working yourself
to death at something you love.
G.B. SHAW

A house divided against itself cannot stand.
ABRAHAM LINCOLN

You only live once, but if you work it right, once is
enough.
JOE E. LEWIS

Men die of fright and live of confidence.
THOREAU

The only place where success comes
before work is in the dictionary.
ANON.

Fortune favors the bold.
VIRGIL

A man is not old until regrets take the place of dreams.
J.D. BARRYMORE

It is easy to take liberty for granted
when you have never had it taken from you.
DICK CHENEY

Nothing in fine print is ever good news.
ANDY ROONEY

Useless laws weaken the necessary laws.
MONTIESQIEU

Talent is a flame. Genius is a fire.
KEN S. KEYES JR.

To be upset over what you don't have is to waste what you do have.
KEN S. KEYES JR.

Getting people to like you
is only the other side of liking them.
N.V. PEALE

If you haven't any charity in your heart,
you have the worst kind of heart trouble.
BOB HOPE

The hardest victory is victory over self.
ARISTOTLE

Self - pity is our worst enemy, if we yield to it, we can never do anything in this world.
HELEN KELLER

Keep cool - even the strongest steel losses it's temper when it is over - heated.
JOE CLARK

Not everything that is faced can be changed. But nothing can be changed until it is faced.
JAMES BALDWIN

When the legend becomes fact, print the legend.
LIBERTY VALANCE

If you believe in God and you're wrong you lose nothing. If you don't believe in God and you're wrong, you've got a big problem.
ANON.

You imagine yourself right in the center of things, and you succeed every time.
JERRY WEST

My biggest fear in life is to be average.
M. NIGHT SHYAMLAN

You can't recharge your batteries by doing nothing. Somewhere, somehow you've got to plug yourself in.
MARILYN VON SAVANT

A dream is a wish
your heart makes when you're fast asleep.
CINDERELLA

Laughter is our defense against the universe.
MEL BROOKS

He deserves a paradise
who can make his companions laugh.
KORAN

The tragedy of life is not so much what we suffer but
rather what we miss.
JOEL WEINTRAUB

There ain't a horse that can't be rode,
there ain't a rider that can't be throwed.
GARY COOPER

Success is living every day of your life in the direction of
your goals, dreams, and ideals.

Successful people live their dreams.

Goal - setting is the first step to all achievement.

If we continue doing the same things, in the same way,
we will get the same results.
JIM CALLAHAN

Life is a live performance, there are no dress rehearsals.
ANON.

To live in the hearts we leave behind is not to die.
HAROLD ROBBINS

Anything the mind can conceive and believe, it can
achieve.
MARCUS AURELIUS

Character should be the standard of excellence.
PAUL ROBESON

It could make a stone cry.
NIKITA KHRUSHCHEV

Don't ever let the facts ruin a good story.
LARRY ANDERSON

Muhammad - Peace be upon him.
The first word revealed to the prophet Muhammad was the verb meaning read.
The first thing created by Allah was the intellect.

The ink of the scholar is more holy than the blood of a martyr.

One learned person is harder on the devil than a thousand ignorant worshipers.

A Muslim submits to the will of Allah.

Taqwa - fear of Allah.

Sunnah - traditions and sayings of the prophet.
MUHAMMAD

You can't win it, if you ain't in it.
TAVIS SMILEY

Quality of life is not a gift, it must be earned.
ROGER SCHWAB

The great masses of the people… Will more easily fall victim to a great lie than a small one.
HITLER

The ages are equal, but genius is always above it's age.
WILLIAM BLAKE

To be loved is to be fortunate, but to be hated is to achieve distinction.
MINNA ANTRIM

It takes twenty years to build a reputation and five minutes to ruin it.
WARREN BUFFET

Every person is a fool in somebody's opinion.
SPANISH PROVERB

Doubt is often the beginning of wisdom.
M. SCOTT PECK

If the enemy within is under control, the enemy without can do you no harm.
AFRICAN PROVERB

We meant to change a nation and instead we changed the world.
RONALD REAGAN

Most children play at being soldiers; it's the ones that never grow up that tend to become generals.
CLAUDE LEWIS

I consider each day a bonus.
MAX PATKIN

The man who sings, chases away his ills.
CERVANTES

I love being rich. It makes me feel all cheery inside.
GERTRUDE STEIN

Never ignore an inner voice that tells you something could be better, even when other people tell you it's O.K.
FRANK SINATRA

Carbon is to steel what perseverance is to character.
ANON.

The only virtue is loyalty.
GEORGE CLOONEY

Doubts are more cruel than the worst of truths.
MOLIERS

When it rains, God is crying.
ANON.

The greater the hunger, the sweeter the sauce.
NAPOLEON

Doubt is the first defeat.
BETH KEPHART

Youth plus alcohol doesn't equal wisdom.
JANN WENNER

The boundaries we establish for our minds are the greatest walls in our lives.
JIM CALLAHAN

Enjoy it, because you never know when it's all going to be taken away.
MICHAEL JORDAN

Character is a diamond that scratches every other stone.
BARTOK

It isn't that they can't see the solution, it is that they can't see the problem.
G.K. CHESTERTON

Talk about others - it's gossip; talk about yourself - it's boring.
ANON.

It's a paradox - Everyone wants a long and happy life,
but no-one wants to get old.
ANDY ROONEY

If you know how rich you are, you are not rich.
IMELDA MARCOS

If anybody has a dream out there,
I'm living proof that it can happen.
KIM BAISINGER

No man is above the law, and no man below it.
TEDDY ROOSEVELT

We are all riding on a limited express.
CARL SANDBURG

Life is made up of moments;
notice and enjoy each and every one.
JIM CALLAHAN

There exists nothing either good or bad
but thinking makes it so.
SHAKESPEARE

The problem with man today is that man doesn't think.
ALBERT SCHWEITZER

If a teacher doesn't think a student can be taught,
he shouldn't be a teacher.
LIV JING HAI

The art of being wise is the art of knowing
what to overlook.
WILLIAM JAMES

Whenever I hear "it can't be done",
I know I'm close to success.
MICHAEL FLATLEY

Success is considered sweetest by those
who never succeed.
EMILY DICKINSON

You have to be like a lion and a fox. A fox to avoid the
traps, a lion to scare away the wolves.
CARLO GAMBINO

If you want to tell people the truth,
you better make them laugh, or they'll kill you.
G.B. SHAW

If you have anything worthwhile to say, dip it in
chocolate so they'll swallow it.
BILLY WILDER

Don't believe everything you think.
ROBERT FULGHAM

We've taken the fun out of the fun,
and the game out of the game.
ANON.

A memory is more indelible than ink.
ANITA LOOS

It is when we all play safe that we create
a world of utmost insecurity.
DAG HAMMERSKJOLD

My lieutenants need only one requirement,
they must be brave.
WELLINGTON

To defeat Napoleon, I recruited the scum of the Earth.
WELLINGTON

He who is hard pressed will regard the greatest daring
as the greatest wisdom.
CLAUSEWITZ

Always be a first - rate version of yourself, instead of a
second - rate version of someone else.
JUDY GARLAND

Everyone like's a good loser, especially when he's on the
opposing team.
MILTON SEGAL

Behind every successful man there's an amazed mother
- in - law.
ANON.

Be wary of the dog that doesn't bark.
A.C. DOYLE

Vengeance leads only to revenge.
DESMOND TUTU

The battle of Waterloo was won on the playing fields of Eton.
WELLINGTON

An army travels on it's stomach.
NAPOLEON

Whenever I speak, I tell the world what I think of myself.
ANON.

Miracles happen quickly and heroes are made in the blink of an eye.
ANON.

Be brief, for no discourse can please when too long.
CERVANTES

It's like they say about life, everything is a lie; you pick out the one you like the best.
MARILYN MANSON

Do not wait for the last judgment. It takes place every day.
ALBERT CAMUS

To be a success you must
master that 3---pound computer between your ears.
MAURER

If you can't excel with talent, triumph with effort.
DAVE WEINBAUM

People seldom become famous for what they say until
after they become famous for what they've done.
CULLEN HIGHTOWER

Truth is something amorphous and vague, highly
malleable to suit the needs of the moment.
JORDANA HORN

We must live as if God does not exist.
DIETRICH BONHOEFFER

If I have only one life to live, let me live it as a lie.
LUC SANTE

Silence is liberty's worst enemy.
TAYLOR GRANT

To live is to suffer, to survive is to find meaning
in the suffering.
GORDON ALLPORT

He who has a why to live can bear with almost any how.
NIETZSCHE

Man is a being who can get used to anything.
DOSTOYEVSKY

Emotion ceases to be suffering as soon as we form a clear and precise picture of it.
SPINOZA

What you have experienced, no power on Earth can take from you.
ANON.

Copernicus - He knew how dangerous it is to be right when the rest of the world is wrong.
THOMAS REED

Don't look at what a person is, but rather at what they can be; and they might become that person.
GOETHE

Change is what keeps you young.
RICK PITINO

You have to be able to laugh at yourself. Otherwise, you suffer.
HELEN KELLER

Music is much too important to be left entirely in the hands of professionals.
ROBERT FULGHUM

The older you get, the more you need people who knew you when you were young.
MARY SCHMICH

Yesterday is but today's memory and tomorrow is today's dream.
KAHLIL GIBRAN

No man is a hero to his valet.
ANON.

We are all in the gutter but some of us are looking at the stars.
OSCAR WILDE

If somebody tells you: "There's nothing to it.", there's a lot more to it.
ANON.

If somebody tells you: "Anybody can do it." Tell them you ain't anybody.
ANON.

A man who wants to lead the orchestra must turn his back to the crowd.
MAX LUCADO

Action is the antidote of despair.
JOAN BAEZ

You can teach only by creating an urge to know.
VICTOR WEISKOPF

It is no simple matter to decide who are the more
fortunate - those to whom life gives all,
or those who have to give all to life.
KUNG SON SOU KY

Sweetest are the uses of adversity.
SHAKESPEARE - GENE TUNNEY

Exercise is a tribute to your heart.
GENE TUNNEY

Success - it can slide away like a coin, or like anything
else on your skin, it can be washed away with soap.
ANDREA BOCELLI

The goal is not to beat Goliath; it is to be Goliath.
MARK WEIDERBOLD

The choice before us is either getting back to the task of
building all children or just keep building more jails.
COLIN POWELL

If our society has lost it's wish for heroes, and it's
capacity to produce them, it may well turn out to have
lost everything else as well.
ARTHUR SCHLESINGER JR.

Shame is the primary cause of all violence.
JAMES GILLIGAN

Courage is grace under pressure.
HEMINGWAY

Permanent war is sold in the guise of patriotism and religion.
JOHN WILKINSON

Listen to the song of life.
KATHERINE HEPBURN

Keep your friends close, but keep your enemies closer.
DON CORLEONE

If I knew I was going to live this long, I would have taken better care of myself.
MICKEY MANTLE

What goes around, comes around. You get what you give.
ANON.

The longest journey is the journey inward.
DAG HAMMARSKJOLD

The greatest pleasure in life is to do a good turn in secret and have it discovered by accident.
ANON.

War is a torture inflicted by foolish old men upon the young.
ANON.

Oh, what a tangled web we weave, when first we practice to deceive.
SIR WALTER SCOTT

Opportunity is missed by most people because it is dressed in overalls and looks like work.
THOMAS EDISON

Chance favors the prepared mind.
LOUIS PASTEUR

A person's mind, stretched by a new idea, can never go back to it's original dimensions.
OLIVER W. HOLMES

With only one behind, you cannot ride on two horses.
GYPSY PROVERB

The last of the laws in learning is repetition.

If you treat everybody alike that's favoritism.

If you're a success, you're the only one that really knows.

If you're a failure, you're the only one that really knows.
JOHN WOODEN

Self confidence is the surest way of obtaining what you want. If you know in your heart you are going to be something, you will be it. . . . . do not permit your mind to think otherwise. It is fatal.
PATTON

It's better to trust and be disappointed once in a while, than to mistrust and be miserable all the time.
ABRAHAM LINCOLN

The worst thing you can do for those you love, is to do things for them they should do for themselves.
ABRAHAM LINCOLN

What a wee little part of a person's life are his acts and his words!
His real life is led in his head, and is known to none but himself. All day long, the mill of his brain is grinding, and his thoughts, not those other things are his history. These are his life, and they are not written, and cannot be written. Everyday would make a whole book of 80,000 words - 365 books a year. Biographies are but the clothes and buttons of the man - the Biography of the man himself cannot be written.
MARK TWAIN

WHAT IT TAKES TO BE NO. 1
BY ROCKY MARCIANO - FORMER UNDEFEATED HEAVYWEIGHT CHAMPION OF THE WORLD

There is no doubt that man is a competitive animal. And there is no place where this fact is more obvious than in the ring. There is no second place. Either you win, or you lose. When they call you champ, it is because you don't lose.

A professional prize fight can last forty-five minutes. That's a long time to keep going. You have to be physically prepared. And you have to be mentally prepared. That means you have to understand pain. There is pain in training. In running that extra mile, when your legs feel like logs. In the dull, monotonous grind, at the light bag and heavy bag. But there's a reason for it. The moment you step into the ring, you know it was worth it. If you've pushed your body into its best shape, there's one thing less to worry about. Maybe it will give you one minute's more stamina. That minute can win you the fight.

Then there's the fear. That's always there. You're not in the ring to demonstrate your courage. You're in there to win the fight. So you handle the fear, maybe even use it. It's out of sight, somewhere behind you, but if you're not completely prepared, it pops up in front of you and then you're finished.

To win takes a commitment of mind and body. When you can't make the commitment, they don't call you champ anymore.

I shall pass this way but once. Any good therefore that I can do or any kindness I can show to any human being, let me do it now. Let me not defer or neglect it, for I shall not pass this way again.
ANON.

"CHILDREN LEARN WHAT THEY LIVE"

If a child lives with criticism, he learns to condemn.
If a child lives with hostility, he learns to fight.
If a child lives with ridicule, he learns to be shy.
If a child lives with shame, he learns to feel guilty.
If a child lives with approval, he learns to like himself.
If a child lives with encouragement, he learns confidence.
If a child lives with praise, he learns to appreciate.
If a child lives with fairness, he learns justice.
If a child lives with security, he learns to have faith.
If a child lives with approval, he learns to like himself.
If a child lives with acceptance and friendship, he learns to find love in the world.

GRANTLAND RICE - THE WAY OF THE MOB

All you who get the cheering and the plaudits from the mob,
Who shrink because they bawl you out upon some off-day job,
Who scowl because they call you names that no one likes to hear,
Who keep the welkin ringing from the horse hoot to the cheer,

Who build you up and knock you down, from here to kingdom come,
Remember as the game goes on - they never boo a bum.
I've heard them hiss Honus Wagner and
I've heard them snarl at Ty Cobb,
I've heard them holler; "Take him out",
with Cristy Matthewson on the job.
I've heard them curse when Babe Ruth struck-out --
or Tris Speaker missed a play.
For forty years I've heard them ride the heroes of their day.
I've heard the roaring welcome switch to something worse than hum,
But Eddie, Ted & Joe get this -- they never boo a bum!

If all mankind minus one were of one opinion, and only one person were of the contrary opinion, mankind would be no more justified in silencing that one person, than he, if he had the power, would be justified in silencing mankind.
JOHN STUART MILL - "ON LIBERTY"

The reasonable man adapts himself to the world; the unreasonable one persists in trying to adapt the world to himself. Therefore all progress depends on the unreasonable man.
G. B. SHAW

There is more to winning than what you see on the field. A team must have character and ambition. It must have soul. Such a team doesn't need a bench packed with stars to win. It will beat a team of superior players who lack the will to win. It will show to its best advantage under pressure. Somehow with the chips down, it will play better than it knows how.
JOE WILLIAMS - BOSTON SPORTSWRITER

Nothing in the world can take the place of persistence.
Talent will not; nothing is more common than the unsuccessful man with talent.
Genius will not; unrewarded genius is almost a proverb.
Education will not; the world is full of educated derelicts.
Persistence and determination are omnipotent.
The slogan 'press on' has solved and always will solve the problems of the human race.
CALVIN COOLIDGE - JOE CLARK

A winner knows how much he still has to learn, even when he is considered an expert by others.
A loser wants to be considered an expert by others, before he has learned enough to know how little he knows.
SYNDEY HARRIS

Resiliency is an important factor in living. The winds of life may bend us, but if we have resiliency of spirit they cannot break us. To courageously straighten again after our heads have been bowed by defeat, disappointment, and suffering is the supreme test of character.
ANON.

POOR RICHARD

Well done is better than said.
Keep conscience clear, than never fear.
Necessity never made a good bargain.
Be slow in choosing a friend, slower in changing.
Wish not so much to live long, as to live well.
Observe all men, thyself first.
Wink at the small faults - remember thou hast great ones.
A lie stands on one leg, truth on two.
Better slip with foot than tongue.
Lost time is never found again.
He that scatters thorns, let him not go barefoot.
BEN FRANKLIN

Drops of water will hollow out a stone.
Never think that you have made any progress until you consider yourself to be inferior to all.
Time must be left to time.
Give all, but without expectation or hope of recompense.
In my life I have always sought for last place.
The ambitious are the most ridiculous and the most pitiful creatures on the earth.
My bags are always packed.
Life isn't a beauty contest.
Born poor and died poor.
POPE JOHN XXIII

GHANDI - MAHATMA   SEVEN DEADLY SINS

Pleasure without conscience, knowledge without character, commerce without morality, science without humanity, worship without sacrifice and politics without principle.

BIBLE SAYINGS

Loves cures people - the ones who give and the ones who receive.
When you judge others, you are revealing your own fears.
If you blame others for our failures, do you credit them with your successes?
Anger is a wind that blows out the lamp of the mind.
Every time you give a piece of your mind, you add to your vacuum.
When you stretch the truth, people usually see through it.
Honesty is the first chapter in the book of wisdom.
Guilt weighs you down. God forgives you, forgive yourself.
Worry is often imagination misplaced.
Never, never, never give up! At the end of your rope? Tie a knot and hang on!
If you can't control the length of your life, you can control its quality.
There are no detour signs along a straight and narrow path.
Some 'open minds' should be closed for repairs.
If you don't stand for something, you fall for anything.
Ruts lead to depression.
The day you can laugh at yourself, is the day you grow up.
There is never a wrong time to do the right thing.

The Man in the Arena

It is not the critic who counts;
Not the man who points out how the strong man stumbles...
The credit belongs to the man who is actually in the arena.
Whose face is marred by dust and sweat and blood;
Who strives valiantly;...
if he fails,
At least he fails while daring greatly.
So that his place shall never be with those cold and timid souls
Who know neither victory nor defeat.
TEDDY ROOSEVELT

Any game, in the beginning, is a bunch of young boys trying to act as grown men; and at its highest point is a bunch of grown men trying to act like a bunch of young boys.
LOU GEHRIG

Nothing can stop the man with the right mental attitude from achieving his goal; nothing on earth can help the man with the wrong mental attitude.
THOMAS JEFFERSON

You don't have to be positive, you just have to be yourself.
You cannot control without being controlled.
The angry people are those who are most afraid.
The thing we run from is the thing we run to.

Consciously or unconsciously, you always get what you expect.
Others can stop you temporarily, only you can do it permanently.
When you blame others, you give up your power to change.
ROBERT ANTHONY

It has always been my thought that the most important single ingredient to success in athletics or life is discipline. I have many times felt that this word is the most ill-defined in all our language. My definition of the word is as follows: 1. Do what has to be done; 2. When it has to be done; 3. As well as it can be done; and 4. Do it that way all the time.
BOBBY KNIGHT

We need to know where we are going, and how we plan to get there. Our dreams and aspirations must be translated into real and tangible goals, with priorities and a time frame. All of this should be in writing, so that it can be reviewed, updated and revised as necessary.
MERLIN OLSEN

The resources of the human body and soul, physical, mental and spiritual, are enormous and beyond our present knowledge and expectations. We go part of the way to consciously tapping these resources by having goals that we want desperately.
HERB ELLIOTT

When fans watch me hit, they think the game must have been easy for me. But it wasn't. I worked very hard to get where I am. For four years, I came to the parks early and worked with our batting coach, Charlie Lau. There were a lot of things I could have done, and probably would have done, but I knew that if I was going to become successful in baseball, I had to do it; I had to work on it.
GEORGE BRETT

HINDU PROVERBS

Even a single lion can tear to pieces a herd of elephants.

You can wake a man who is asleep, but not a man who is awake.

Great heat at the beginning ruins grand projects.

Stick to one thing and all will come; aim at everything and all will go.

Everything can be taken from a person but one thing:
The last of the freedoms -
To choose one's attitude in any given set of circumstances,
to choose one's own way.
VICTOR FRANKL

Look to this day for yesterday is but a dream
and tomorrow is only a vision,

but today, well lived makes every yesterday a dream of happiness and every tomorrow a vision of hope. Look well, therefore, to this day.
SANSKRIT PROVERB

Every morning you are handed 24 golden hours. They are one of the few things in this world you get free of charge. If you had all the money in the world you could not buy an extra hour. What will you do with this priceless treasure? Remember, you must use it, as it is given only once.
SHANYNE MARCHAND 16 YR. OLD

I desire to go to Hell, not to Heaven. In Hell I shall enjoy the company of Popes, Kings and Princes, but in Heaven are only Beggars, Monks, Hermits and Apostles.
MACHIAVELLI

Queen Elizabeth the First was the richest, most powerful woman in the world. On her deathbed she had only one request: "All my possessions for a moment of time" - Her request was denied.
ANON.

Be careful of the words you speak ---
keep them soft and sweet
for you never know from day to day
which ones you'll have to eat.
ANON.

If we discovered that we had only five minutes left to say all we wanted to say, every telephone would be occupied by people calling other people to say that they loved them.
CHRISTOPHER MORLEY

It's not what you eat, but what you digest that makes you strong;
it's not what you earn, but what you save that makes you rich,
it's not what you learn, but what you remember that make you wise.
CHINESE PROVERB

The man who views the world at <u>fifty</u>,
the same as he did at <u>twenty</u>,
has wasted thirty years of his life.
MUHAMMAD ALI

Heroes are remembered,
But legends never die.
Follow your heart and you can't
go wrong, -- think about it kid.
THE SANDLOT
J. E. JONES

I believe the one idea, factor, strength, skill, force, experience, or motivation that has helped me most in achieving success has been my use or exertion of self-discipline.
LEE TREVINO

The successful man has enthusiasm. Good work is never done in cold blood; heat is needed to forge anything. Every great achievement is the story of a flaming heart.
HARRY S. TRUMAN

Every man is enthusiastic at times. One man has enthusiasm for 30 minutes, another for 30 days, but it is the man who has it for 30 years who makes a success of his life.
EDWARD B. BUTLER, SCIENTIST

Fame and fortune haven't gone to my head. I just try to enjoy life, and have a little fun. As for basketball, I want to have fun. Jump up and down and scream. I love to play basketball.
EARVIN "MAGIC" JOHNSON

My father taught me you can't spend any time worrying about whether you're going to lose. You can't measure success if you've never failed.
STEFFI GRAF

Never tell a young person that something cannot be done. God may have been waiting for centuries for somebody ignorant enough of the impossible to do that thing.
DR. J. A. HOLMES

If I do not practice one day, I know it. If I do not practice the next, the orchestra knows it. If I do not practice the third day, the whole world knows it.
IGNACE PADEREWESKI

Before I get into the ring, I have already won or lost out on the road. The real part is won or lost somewhere far away from witnesses -- and behind the lines, in the gym and out there on the road long before I dance under those lights.
MUHAMMAD ALI

I don't care how great a player is, if he is not a team player, he isn't going to help you much, and the chances are he won't help you at all when you need help the most.
JOE WILLIAMS
BOSTON SPORTSCASTER

Doing things out of obligation, no matter how much effort you put into it, will always be like dragging a ball and chain. Because of this, every man should struggle to love what he does when he cannot do what he loves.
BLANCO Y NEGRO

Winning is like being on a tightrope. If you look down, you'll get dizzy and fall. If you look up, some team will come the other way and knock you off. If you look straight ahead and stay focused, you've got a chance.
CHUCK NOLL

Money may be the husk of many things, but not the kernel. It brings you food, but not appetite; medicine, but not health; acquaintances, but not friends; servants, but not loyalty; days of joy, but not peace or happiness.
IBSEN

Furthermore, I had been surprised to find out that the more championships you win, the more criticism you receive, the more suspicious people are of you, the more there is expected of you, the less appreciation there is of what has been accomplished, and the less personal satisfaction you have.
JOHN WOODEN

Class. You can't beg, borrow or buy it. If you go out looking for it, you'll never find it. Class isn't the money you make, the clothes you wear, the car you drive, or the house you live in. It isn't the way you pronounce your vowels, cross your legs, or fold your napkin. It isn't the people you know or the places you go. Class either is, or it isn't.
LARRY KEITH - SPORT'S ILLUSTRATED

A FRIEND

What is a friend? I will tell you. It is a person with whom you dare to be yourself. Your soul can be naked with him. He seems to ask you to put on nothing, only to be what you are. He does not want you to be better or worse. When you are with him, you feel as a prisoner feels who has been declared innocent. You do not have to be on your guard. You can say what you think, so long as it is genuinely you. He understands those contradictions in your nature that lends others to misjudge you. With him you breathe freely. You can avow your little vanities and envies and hates and vicious sparks, your meanesses, and absurdities and in opening them up to him, they are lost, dissolved on the white ocean of his loyalty. He understands. You do not have to be careful. You can abuse him, neglect him, tolerate him. Best of all, you can keep still with him. It makes no matter. He likes you. ---He is like fire that purges to the bone. He understands. You can weep with him, sing with him, laugh with him, pray with him. Through it all - and underneath - he sees, knows and loves you. A friend? What is a friend? Just one, I repeat, with whom you dare to be yourself.

RAYMOND BERAN

FOR CHARITY

Keep us, o God, from all pettiness. Let us be large in thought, in word, in deed. Let us be done with fault - finding and leave off all self - seeking.
May we put away all pretense and meet each other face to face, without self - pity and without prejudice.
May we never be hasty in judgment, and always be generous.
Let us always take time for all things, and make us to grow calm, serene, and gentle. Teach us to put into action our better impulses, to be straightforward and unafraid. Grant that we may realize that it is the little things of life that create differences, that in the big things of life, we are as one. And, O Lord God, let us not forget to be kind! Amen.

MARY STUART

Decisions

If you decide you are beaten, you are.
If you decide you dare not, you don't.
If you'd like to win, but decide you can't, you won't.
If you decide you'll lose, you've lost, for out in the world you'll find
success begins with a person's will, think big and your deeds will grow, think small and you fall behind.
Decide that you can and you will, it's all in the state of mind.
If you think you're outclassed, you are.
You've gotta think win to rise, you have to be sure of yourself, before you can claim the prize.
Life's battle doesn't always go to the stronger or faster man, but sooner or later the one who wins, is the one that decides he can.

ANON.

Yesterday - Today - Tomorrow

There are two days in every week about which we should not worry, two days which should be kept free from fear and apprehension.

One of these days is yesterday with it's mistakes and cares, it's fault and blunders, it's aches and pains. Yesterday has passed forever beyond our control. All money in the world cannot bring back yesterday. We cannot undo a single act we performed; we cannot erase a single word we said…….. yesterday is gone. The other day we should not worry about is tomorrow with it's possible adversaries, it's burdens, it's large promise and poor performance. Tomorrow is also beyond our immediate control. Tomorrow's sun will rise, either in splendor or in a mask of clouds, but it will rise. Until it does, we have no stake in tomorrow, for it is yet unborn.

This leaves only one day……Today. Any person can fight the battle of just one day. It is only when you and I add the burden of these two awful eternities……Yesterday and Tomorrow that we break down.

It is not the experience of today that drives men mad - it is remorse or bitterness for something which happened yesterday and the dread of what tomorrow may bring.

Let us, therefore, live but one day at a time!!!

UNKNOWN

For Whom The Bell Tolls

No man is an Island, entire of itself; every man is a piece of the continent, a part of the main. If a clod be washed away by the sea, Europe is the less, as well as if a promontary were, as well as if a manor of thy friend's or of thine own were: any man's death diminishes me, because I am involved in mankind, and therefore never send to know for whom the bell tolls; it tolls for thee.

JOHN DONNE

RISKS

To laugh is to risk appearing the fool.
To weep is to risk appearing sentimental.
To reach out for another is to risk involvement.
To expose feelings is to risk exposing your true self.
To place your ideas, your dreams before a crowd is to risk their loss.
To love is to risk not being loved in return.
To live is to risk dying.
To hope is to risk despair.
To try is to risk failure.
But risks must be taken, because the greatest hazard in life is to risk nothing.
The person who risks nothing, does nothing, has nothing and is nothing.
They may avoid suffering and sorrow but they cannot learn, feel, change, grow, love, live.
Chained by their certitude they are a slave, they have forfeited their freedom.
Only a person who risks is free.

DALE CARNEGIE

When we hate our enemies, we give them power over us - power over our sleep, our appetites and our happiness. They would dance with joy, if they knew how much they were worrying us. Our hate is not hurting them at all, but it is turning our own days and nights into hellish turmoil.
DALE CARNEGIE

Just For Today

Just for today I will try to live through this day only, and not tackle my whole life problem at once. I can do something for twelve hours that would appall me if I felt that I had to keep it up for a lifetime.

Just for today I will be happy. This assumes to be true what Abraham Lincoln said, that, "Most folks are as happy as they make up their minds to be."

Just for today I will adjust myself to what is, and not try to adjust everything to my own desires. I will take my "luck" as it comes, and fit myself to it.

Just for today I will try to strengthen my mind. I will study. I will learn something useful. I will not be a mental loafer. I will read something that requires effort, thought, and concentration.

Just for today I will exercise my soul in three ways; I will do somebody a good turn, and not get found out; if anybody knows of it, it will not count, I will do at least two things I don't want to do, just for exercise. I will not show anyone that my feelings are hurt; they may be hurt, but today I will not show it.

Just for today I will be agreeable. I will look as well as I can, dress becomingly, act courteously, criticize not one bit, not find fault with anything, and not try to improve or regulate anybody except myself.

Just for today I will have a program. I may not follow it exactly, but I will have it. I will save myself from two pests: hurry and indecision.

Just for today I will have a quiet half hour all by myself and relax. During this half hour, sometime, I will try to get a better perspective of my life.

Just for today I will be unafraid. Especially I will not be afraid to enjoy what is beautiful, and to believe that as I give to the world, so the world will give to me.

UNKNOWN

I believe only one person in a thousand knows the trick of really living in the present. Most of us spend 59 minutes an hour living in the past with regret for lost joys, or shame for things badly done (both utterly useless and weakening) or in a future which we either long for or dread. The only way to live is to accept each minute as an unrepeatable miracle, which is exactly what it is - a miracle and unrepeatable.

STORM JAMESON

ANYWAY

People are unreasonable, illogical, and self-centered, love them anyway.

If you do good people will accuse you of selfish, ulterior motives. Do good anyway.

If you are successful, you'll win false friends and true enemies, succeed anyway.

The good you do today will be forgotten tomorrow. Do good anyway.

Honesty and frankness make you vulnerable, be honest and frank anyway.

People favor underdogs but follow top dogs. Fight for some underdogs anyway.

What you spend years building may be destroyed overnight. Build anyway.
People really need help but may attack you if you help them. Help people anyway.
Give the world the best you have and you'll get kicked in the teeth. Give the world the best you've got, anyway.
ANON.

TO "LET GO" TAKES LOVE

To "let go" does not mean to stop caring, it means I can't do it for someone else. To "let go" is not to cut myself off, it is the realization I can't control another. To "let go" is not to enable, but to allow learning from natural consequences. To "let go" is to admit powerlessness, which means the outcome is not in my hands. To "let go" is not to try to change or blame another, it is to make the most of myself. To "let go" is not to care for, but to care about. To "let go" is not to fix, but to be supportive. To "let go" is not to judge, but to allow another to be a human being. To "let go" is not to be in the middle arranging all the outcomes, but to allow others to affect their own destinies. To "let go" is not to be protective, it is to permit another to face reality. To "let go" is not to deny, but accept. To "let go" is not to nag, scold, or argue, but instead to search out my own shortcomings, and to correct them. To "let go" is to not adjust everything to my own desires, but to take each day as it comes, and to cherish myself in. To "let go" is not to criticize and regulate anybody, but to try to become what I dream I can be. To "let go" is to not regret the past, but to grow and live for the future.
To "let go" is to fear less and to love more.
ANON.

DON'T QUIT

When things go wrong, as they sometimes will,
When the road you're trudging seems all uphill,
When the funds are low and the debts are high,
And you want to smile, but you have to sigh,
When care is pressing you down a bit-
Rest if you must, but don't you quit.

Life is funny with its twists and turns,
As every one of us sometimes learns,
And many a fellow turns about
When he might have won had he stuck it out.
Don't give up though the pace seems slow-
You may succeed with another blow.

Often the goal is nearer than
It seems to a faint and faltering man;
Often the struggler has given up
When he might have captured the victor's cup;
And he learned too late when the night came down,
How close he was to the golden crown.

Success is failure turned inside out-
The silver tint of the clouds of doubt,
And you never can tell how close you are,
It may be near when it seems afar;
So stick to the fight when you're hardest hit-
It's when things seem worst that you mustn't quit.

ANON.

TO BE NO. 1

The difference between a successful man and others is not a lack of strength, not a lack of knowledge, but rather a lack of will, because the character rather than education is man's greatest need and man's greatest safeguard, because the character is higher than the intellect. The difference betwcen men is in energy, in the strong will, in a singleness of purpose and an invincible determination. But the great difference is in sacrifice, in self - denial, in love and loyalty, in fearlessness and humility, in the pursuit of excellence and in the perfectly disciplined will, because this is not only the difference between men, this is the difference between great and little men.
V. T. LOMBARDI

You are always my friend
when I am happy
or when I am sad
when I am all alone
of when I am with people
You are always my friend
if I see you today
or if I see you a year from now
if I talk to you today
or if I talk to you a year from now
You are always my friend...
and though through the years
we will change
it doesn't matter what I do
it doesn't matter what you do
Throughout our lifetime
you are always my friend
SUSAN POLIS SCHULZ

WAIT
(Written by a Russian Soldier to his wife during the Battle of Stalingrad)

Wait for me, and I'll return. Only wait very hard.
Wait when you are filled with sorrow as you watch the yellow rain.
Wait, when the wind sweeps the snowdrifts.
Wait in the sweltering heat.
Wait when other have stopped waiting, forgetting their yesterday.
Wait, even when from afar no letters come to you.
Wait, even when others are tired of waiting.
Wait, even when my mother and son think I am no more.
And when my friends sit around the campfire, drinking to my memory,
Wait and do not hurry to drink to my memory too.
Wait, for I'll return, defying every dare.
And let those that did not wait, say that I was lucky.
They will never understand that in the midst of death, you with your waiting saved me.
Only you and I will know how I survived.
It is because you waited when no - one else did.

Tell Him Now
If with pleasure you are viewing
Any work a man is doing;
If you like him, or you love him, tell him now.
Don't withhold your approbation
Till the parson makes oration
And he lies with snowy lilies o'er his brow.
For no matter how you shout it,
He won't really care about it,
He won't really know how many tear - drops you have shed.

If you think some praise is due him,
Now's the time to slip it to him,
For he cannot read his tombstone when he's dead!
UNKNOWN

IT'S IN YOUR FACE

You don't have to tell how you live each day,
You don't have to say if you work or you play,
A tried, true barometer serves in the place
However you live, it will show in your face.
The false, the deceit you bear in your heart
Will not stay inside, where it first got a start,
For sinew and blood are a thin veil of lace,
What you wear in your heart is what you wear in your face.
If your life is unselfish, if for others you live
For not what you get, but for how much you can give,
If you live close to God, in His infinite grace,
You don't have to tell it, it shows in your face.
UNKNOWN

That man is a success, who has lived well, laughed often, and loved much; who has gained the respect of intelligent men and the love of children; who has filled his life and accomplished his task; who leaves the world better than he found it, whether by an improved flower, a perfect poem or a rescued soul; who never lacked appreciation of Earth's beauty or failed to express it; who looked for the best in others and gave the best he had.
DALE CARNEGIE

The Measure Of A Man

Not - "How did he die?" But - "How did he live?"
Not - "What did he gain?" But - "What did he give?"
These are the units to measure the worth
Of a man as a man, regardless of birth.
Not - "What was his station?" But - "Had he a heart?"
And - "How did he play his God - given part?
Was he ever ready with a word of good cheer,
To bring back a smile, to banish a tear?"
Not - "What was his church?" Nor - "What was his creed?"
But - "Had he befriended those really in need?"
Not - "What did the sketch in the newspaper say?"
But - "How many were sorry when he passed away?"
UNKNOWN

You are richer today than you were yesterday, if you have laughed often, given something, forgiven even more, made a new friend, made stepping stones out of stumbling blocks; if you have thought more in terms of "thyself" than "myself" or if you have managed to be cheerful even if you were weary.
AUTHOR UNKNOWN

You do not need to strain,
You do not need to force anything, only be.
Be quiet in mind, in manner, in movement, cultivate quietness.
Let there be an aura of quietness surrounding thee.
Eliminate all unnecessary anxiety, and let the power of spirit take over.
Remember, tranquillity, serenity, strength and a gentleness born of deep confidence in God's love over - ruling all for good.

Let nothing disturb thee, nothing afright thee. All things are working together for good. All things are passing. God will not leave thee.
ENA HOLMSTY

Winning isn't everything, but the will to win is. The will to excel and the will to win, are positive, enduring factors. They are more important than any events that occasion them. We have to pay the price. We live in an age when the prizes and the perils never have been so great. All too often we confuse freedom with license, forgetting what is all - important - duty, respect for authority and mental discipline. We need more than engineers and scientists. We need people with wisdom and courage. Leaders were made, not born - mental discipline, humility, spartanism, dedication, sacrifice, self - denial, loyalty, fearlessness and love. I mean the love of one man for the dignity of another, I am talking about "heart power", because battles are won in the hearts of men while "hate power", is the weakness of the world.
VINCE LOMBARDI

No Indispensable Man
Sometime when you're feeling important,
Sometime your egos in bloom.
Sometime when you take it for granted
Your the most qualified man in the room,

Sometime when you feel that you're going,
Would leave an unfillable hole,

Just follow the directions below and see
How, it really humbles the soul.

Take a bucket and fill it with water,
Put your hand in up to your wrist,
Take it out and the hole that's remaining
Is the measure of how much you'll be missed.

You can splash all about as you enter.
You can stir up the water galore,
when you stop, in less than a minute,
It's the same as it was before.

There's a moral to this quaint example
Just do the best you can,
Be good to yourself - but remember -
There is no Indispensable Man.

ANON.

Talent must not be wasted… Those who have talent must hug it, embrace it, nurture it and share it, lest it is taken away from you as fast as it was loaned to you.
Trust me. I've been there.
FRANK SINATRA

PARADOX

I asked God for strength, that I might achieve…….
I was made weak, that I may learn humbly to obey.

I asked for health, that I might do greater things…….
I was given infirmity, that I might do better things.

I asked for riches, that I might be happy…….
I was given poverty, that I might be wise.

I asked for power, that I might have the praise of men…….
I was given weakness, that I might feel the need of God.

I asked for all things, that I might enjoy life.
I was given life, that I might enjoy all things.

I got nothing that I asked for, but everything that I had hoped for.
Almost despite myself, my unspoken prayers were answered, I am , among all, most richly blessed!

Talent is not only a blessing, it is a burden.

Teams do not go physically flat, but they go mentally stale.

The harder you work, the harder it is to lose (surrender).
Success is paying the price.
You have got to pay the price to win—
To get there, to stay there.

The will is character in action.

The successful man is honest with himself.

If we constantly dwell upon the errors, then failure becomes the goal.

Prosperity is a great teacher, adversity is greater.

Mental toughness is essential to success.

Once you learn to quit, it becomes a habit.

Defeat is education, the first step to something better.
Do not be afraid of defeat.

A disciplined person is one who follows the will of the one who gives the orders.
Let's make molehills out of mountains and not mountains out of molehills.

The difference between success and failure is energy.

VINCE LOMBARDI

Ninety-five percent of the people in this world go to their graves never getting to do what makes them happy.
SPIKE LEE

What you failed to do, destroys you.
JIMMY BRESLIN

There are no shortcuts to any place worth going.
BEVERLY SILLS

Becoming number one is a lot easier than remaining number one.
SENATOR BILL BRADLEY

Everybody wants to go to heaven but nobody wants to die.
JOE LOUIS

The strongest steel survives the fire.
BILL CONNOLLY JR.

Failure is an opportunity to begin again, more intelligently.
HENRY FORD

If it was easy, there would be a lot of people doing it.
MARK McGWIRE

If you believe in dreams and you believe in yourself, you can climb the mountain and bust through the walls.
MARK McGWIRE

Just show up for work everyday, you'll be surprised at all you might get done.
CAL RIPKEN SR. TO CAL RIPKEN JR.

Sometimes, you don't realize the greatest moments of your lifetime while they're happening. You think there will be other times.
FIELD OF DREAMS

A man is fortunate if he can meet even the shadow of a friend.
JIMMY BRESLIN

It's a lot easier to start something than it is to finish it.
AMELIA EARHART

The most valuable of all talents is that of never using two words when one will do.
THOMAS JEFFERSON

He who permits himself to tell a lie once, finds it much easier to do it a second time.
THOMAS JEFFERSON

Injustice anywhere is a threat to justice everywhere.
MARTIN LUTHER KING

War is a poor chisel to carve out tomorrow.
MARTIN LUTHER KING

Am I not destroying my enemies when I make friends of them.

It has been my experience that folks who have no vices have very few virtues.

I don't think much of a man who is not wiser today than he was yesterday.
ABRAHAM LINCOLN

You cannot shake hands with a clenched fist.
GOLDA MEIR

Don't be humble; you're not that great.
GOLDA MEIR

Creditors have better memories than debtors.
BEN FRANKLIN

Blessed is he who expects nothing, for he shall never be disappointed.
BEN FRANKLIN

Anyone who stops learning is old, anyone who keeps learning stays young.

My best friend is the one who brings out the best in me.

Don't find fault, find a remedy.
HENRY FORD

There is no god higher than truth.

Non-violence is the first article of faith.

Cowards can never be moral.

Honest differences are often a healthy sign of progress.
GANDHI

In great attempts it is glorious even to fail.
VINCE LOMBARDI

Whether you're rich or poor, it always pays to have money.
BEN RABINOWITZ

Three may keep a secret, if two of them are dead.
BEN FRANKLIN

Forgiveness is not an occasional act; it is a permanent attitude.
MARTIN LUTHER KING

The great enemy of clear language is insincerity.
GEORGE ORWELL

To a beautiful woman; hell is growing old.
RUSSIAN PROVERBS

All the flowers of all the tomorrows are in the seeds of today.
ANON.

Life is a party. You should come to the table and eat your fill.
PAMELA HARRIMAN

The only time you don't want to fail is the last time you try.
CHAS. KETTERING

The sin is to become predictable.
MIKE PETTINE

I cant's wait until tomorrow, because I get better looking every day.
JOE NAMATH

The good old days are tomorrow.
JOHN QUINN

Everybody makes mistakes, nobody's perfect.
SAMMY SOSA

Positive thoughts are really prayers in disguise.
ANON.

A lie unravels you.
ALICE WALKER

If you want'em, you can't have'em. If you have'em, you don't want'em.
GEORGE GERSHWIN

The happy childhood is hardly worth your while.
FRANK McCOURT

Live life like you're going to live forever, not like you're going to die tomorrow.
W. BURNETT

I've never seen no ugly wins.
BILL SPIERS—ASTROS

The best part about baseball is no homework.
DAN QUISENBERRY

Playing baseball everyday was like Christmas.
DAN QUISENBERRY

If I felt I didn't put all my effort in, I couldn't look in the mirror.
MO VAUGHAN

The greatest of all human adventures is the quest for self-knowledge.
GILBERT WADBAUER

People may change the sky above their head when they cross the ocean but not their spirit.
HORACE -65 B.C.

No matter how bad my life was or how disconnected I felt from my family, I never felt that my life meant nothing.
OPRAH WINFREY

Winning comes down to playing smart.
SONNY JURGENSEN

The chains had been taken off my legs and placed around my mind.
WILLIAM CAMPBELL

Events do not change us they reveal us to ourselves.
M. R. THON

Forgiveness is a true sign of power: Revenge is a true sign of weakness.
ANON

You think you destroy the thing you love, but you find out the thing you love destroys you.
MUHAMMAD ALI

Before 40 a person has the face he was born with, after 40 he has the face he deserves.
DAVID FINKLE

There is a moment for all of us, If you do not give up, you will reach it.
FLORENCE GRIFFITH JOYNER

As a kid you spend years gripping a baseball, as you grow older you realize it's been just the opposite.
JIM BOUTON

Let our revenge be the laughter of our children.
BOBBY SANDS

We have within us a wise physician.
ALBERT SCHWIETZER

Failure is an opportunity to begin again, more intelligently.
HENRY FORD

A gentleman never kisses and tells.
EAROL FLYNN

Leadership: Getting someone else to do something you want done because he wants to do it.
DWIGHT D. EISENHOWER

Don't con the con man.
ANON.

People want to see the dark side.
TEDDY ATLAS

One of the keys to living fully is imagination, it allows us to escape the predictable.
SEN. BILL BRADLEY

The total of all the minds in the universe equals one mind.
ANON.

It is a big river, indeed, that cannot be crossed.
MAORI PROVERB

A pint of sweat will save a gallon of blood.
PATTON

Behind teenage drug use is an unhappy, empty heart.
PATRICK FAGAN

It's a shame, 99% of the lawyers give the rest of them a bad name.
ANON.

One of the reasons we're here is to discover the reason we're here.
GERRY MCOSCAR

Gold covers a host of character flaws.
ED VOVES

Only the dead have seen the end of war.
PLATO

God can dream a bigger dream for you than you can dream for yourself.
OPRAH WINFREY

The stage is not a place for the faint of heart.
JIMMY BUFFETT

The fastest method of overcoming obstacles is the team method.
COLIN L. POWELL

Resentment is like taking poison
and waiting for the other person to die.
MALACHY McCOURT

Memory is better than a video because, it's free and it
doesn't work very well.
DAVID OWEN

Fear is faith that won't work out.
SISTER MARY TRICKY

When a team plays without passion, the game becomes
boring.
BARBARA DE ANGELIS

To be prepared for war is one of the most effective ways
of preserving peace.
GEORGE WASHINGTON

In spite of everything I still believe that people are
really good at heart.
ANNE FRANK

The strongest thing baseball has going for it today is
yesterday.
LAWRENCE RITTER

There are two places in this league, first place and no
place.
TOM SEAVER

Baseball is like church, many attend
but few understand.
WES WESTRUM

They never boo a bum.
GRANTLAND RICE

Publicity is like poison—it only hurts if you swallow it.
JOE PATERNO

The main obligation is to amuse yourself.
S. J. PERLEMAN

The building of castles in the air, made architects of us
all.
GENE FOWLER

People are hungry because their voices are not heard in
the halls of power.
ANON.

America is a great bubble that has to burst.
GENE FOWLER

Being powerful is like being a lady, if you have to tell
people you are, you aren't.
MARGARET THATCHER

If you can't convince them, confuse them.
HARRY TRUMAN

ON SPORTS:
When the shower begins to feel better than the workout, it's time to give it up.

ON COACHING:
The hours are long, the pay is short but it's great for its insecurity.
BILL WALSH
NOTRE DAME LINE COACH

The future is not what you inherit but what you create. Little decisions are made with your head, big decisions are made with your heart.

Life is not holding good cards but playing a poor hand well
K. S. BHARGAVA

Politics is too serious a matter to be left to the politicians.
De GAULLE

For glory gives herself only to those who have always dreamed of her.
De GAULLE

I think and think for months and years. Ninety-nine times the conclusion is false. The one-hundredth time I am right.
ALBERT EINSTEIN

Sometimes one pays most for the thing one
gets for nothing.
ALBERT EINSTEIN

Leadership: getting someone else to do something you
want done because he wants to do it.
DWIGHT D. EISENHOWER

Brains are no substitute for judgement.
DEAN ACHENSON

Sometimes you have to make arguments
clearer than the truth.
DEAN ACHENSON

No ones moment last forever.
JAYSON STARK

Democracy the worst form of government
devised by man—
Until you consider all others.
WINSTON CHURCHILL

Let me hang myself with my own words. I don't want
someone else to hang me with theirs.
EVANDER HOLYFIELD

You always have to be vigilant,
always have to push the envelope.
BILLIE JEAN KING

I knew what my destiny was. I wanted to play tennis.
BILLIE JEAN KING

I had to create a place to go.
BILLIE JEAN KING

SAYINGS OF DAMON RUNYON

I love people who steal.

I never bite the hand that feeds me.

Never give a sucker an even break.

All horse players die broke.

I ride winners only.

The worst of all crimes, that of being boring.

Favorites only can win, when they can win.

Never knock a winner.

The payroll is a more important document than the bible.

Son, there will come a time when you are out in the world and you and you will meet a man that says he can make the jack of hearts spit cider into your ear. Son, even if this man has a brand new deck of cards wrapped in cellophane, do not bet that man, because if you do, you will have a mighty wet ear.
DAMON RUNYON

If I'm gonna get beat, I'm gonna get beat my way.

Victory is one of the best painkillers I've come across.
Money changes everything, but its impact on baseball goes all the way to the bone.
BOB GIBSON

On Bob Gibson
Anybody can pitch when the other team doesn't score any runs.
CURT FLOOD

All the glory comes from daring to begin.
E.F. WARE

Only those who dare to fail greatly can ever achieve greatly.
ANON.

Choice, not chance, determines destiny.
ANON.

Problems are opportunities in work clothes.
HENRY KAISER

Failure to hit the bull's eye is never the fault of the target.
GILBERT ARLAND

Our chief want in life is somebody who will make us do what we can.
RALPH WALDO EMERSON

The road to success is paved with good intentions.
ANON.

We cannot direct the wind... But we can adjust the sails.
ANON.

Act as though it where impossible to fail.
ANON.

People seldom improve when they have no other model but themselves to copy.
GOLDSMITH

Paralyze resistance with persistence.
WOODY HAYES

The price of greatness is responsibility.
WINSTON CHURCHILL

It will be a great day when our schools have all the money they need, and the Air Force has to hold a bake sale to buy a bomber.
WOMENS LEAGUE SLOGAN

Life is not always to take, it is more to give than to take.
LILI BITA

Kids who master reading usually master self-control.
PAUL STEPHENSON

There is no such thing as bad publicity.
NIKOLAI TOLSTOY

I don't give a damn what they write about me;
just so they spell my name correctly.
BETTE DAVIS

If you get success, no matter how small,
no one will ever steal it.
MILOUD OUKILI

Behold the turtle! He makes progress
only when he sticks his neck out.
ANON.

Good habits are just as hard to break as bad habits.
COLLEEN MARIA RAE

A happy family is heaven on earth.
MARY ENGELBREIT

Our strength is what we do for the weakest.
AIDA ALVAREZ

Your ability to keep going and prevail, regardless of the
odds, has to start and end in your heart.
JULIA ROBERTS

The human teenager is the most
vicious animal on earth.
You don't see a pack of wolves
making fun of other wolves.
BRANDI BROWN AGE 17

There is more treasure in books than all the pirates loot
on Treasure Island.
WALT DISNEY

That which does not kill me, makes me stronger.
VICTOR FRANKL

Love without forgiveness was not love to begin with.
KATHIE L. GIFFORD

Nobody is immune to ridicule.
STEVE SESKIN

You may encounter many defeats,
but you must not be defeated.
We can only know where we're going
if we know where we've been.
MAYA ANGELOU

Kids learn from anybody who's teaching them
something they feel they're going to benefit from.
JOHN CHANEY

Good things come to those who wait. The secret
is to be able to wait long enough.

The less you tell people about yourself,
the more interested they become.
ARCHIE MOORE

All things are possible until they are proved impossible -
even the impossible may only be so as of now.
PEARL S. BUCK

I would never belong to any organization that would
have someone like me as a member.
GROUCHO MARX

Ideas are easy. It's execution that's hard.
JEFF BEZOS

To rob a person of his dignity
is the equivalent of murder.
JEWISH LAW

I love antiques, but I don't want to be one.
VIRGINIA GRAHAM

THE STOCK MARKET

With enough inside information and a million dollars,
you will go broke in a year.

The first rule is not to lose.
The second rule is not to forget the first rule.

You try to be greedy when others are fearful,
And fearful when others are greedy.
WARREN BUFFETT

Your emotions are often a reverse indicator of
what you ought to be doing.
JOHN F. HINDELONG

Film is not a career for grown-ups.
BILLY WILDER

God is of no importance unless He is of supreme
importance.
ABRAHAM HESCHEL

You can't be passive and recover from serious illness.
SAM RATMANSKY

Age is nothing but experience, and some of us are more
experienced than others.
MICKEY ROONEY

Every calling is great when greatly pursued.
OLIVER W. HOLMES

Fame is the dubious privilege of being known by the
people who don't know you.
ART CAREY

I like to take a lemon and make lemonade.

We all want the same things in life - to be safe and
healthy, and to have someone to love.
MAYA ANGELOU

All motivation is self - motivation.
SETH GODIN

If I've helped anyone, then I've helped me.
GIRL SCOUTS OF AMERICA

The surest way to lose a friend
is to tell him something for his own good.
SID ASCHER

The wind always blows hardest
at the top of the mountain.
JOHN THOMPSON

A day without an argument is like an egg without salt.
ANGELA CARTER

If I were to choose between pain and nothing,
I would choose pain.
WILLIAM FAULKNER

Everywhere a greater joy is preceded by a greater suffering
ST. AUGUSTINE

Any body can be great because anyone can serve.
MARTIN LUTHER KING

PLEASE START COLLECTING YOUR OWN
FAVORITE QUOTES!

TO BE CONTINUED…

CPSIA information can be obtained
at www.ICGtesting.com
Printed in the USA
BVOW11s2243260916

463391BV00003B/7/P

9 780741 400260